Ultimate Truth

The Science and Philosophy of
Spiritual Evolution and Manifestation

Anthony Peters

WiseMonkeyTraining.co.uk

ISBN: 9781982902483

DEDICATION

With deepest love and gratitude to my wife Helen

CONTENTS

INTRODUCTION

Dr Herbert Benson pulled his thick thermal coat tighter against the cold air of the Himalayas as he watched his team check their equipment.

His attention turned back to the rows of seated Buddhist Monks facing a table dashed with brightly coloured offerings around a large central golden statue of a Buddha. Beautifully adorned in their dark-red and mustard-yellow robes they sat still in meditation. Some were throat chanting, the hypnotic sound filling the temple. The stone walls amplifying the reverberating tone so that the collective and synchronised low-pitched mutterings vibrated in the doctor's chest.

Dr Benson was snapped out of his trance by one of the research team.

"Herbert. Can you give me a hand with this please?"

"Yes, of course. Let's hope this equipment works at this altitude and temperature" Dr Herbert Benson replied before blowing warm breath into his cupped hands.

"Yes, slightly different to our labs at Harvard hey?" said the researcher rhetorically.

An hour later and they were set up. A few preliminary tests indicated all electrodes and measuring devices were working perfectly. The time had come.

The Monks to be studied were amused by the head caps and draping wires attached to various parts of their body but soon the banter and teasing subsided as they settled and prepared to meditate.

The researchers gathered around their monitors as the Monks positioned and readied themselves to fall into a meditative state. It did not take long before dramatic changes in brain waves started to show on Herbert's laptop screen.

From Beta to Alpha brain waves, soon the Monks entered yet another level of mind state as their brain wave length increased into Theta. Herbert and his team marvelled at the Monks ability to control their mind state. It was truly remarkable, but nothing could prepare them for what happened next.

With wooden buckets in hand, some other Monks walked over to those in meditation, fished out soaking wet towels and draped them over each of the meditators.

A few of the researchers looked over at Dr Benson with a wide-eyed facial gesture clearly expressing their concern. At these freezing ambient temperatures, the Monks would surely become hypothermic within minutes. Acknowledging their concerns Herbert looked down at his screen to check the Monks' vital signs. Heart rate, good. Blood pressure, good. Body temperature ...

Conscious of his staring colleagues awaiting reassurance, still transfixed on the information tracking across the screens in front of him, the Doctor waved a 'thumbs up' without raising his head.

He was witnessing significant movement in the Monks' body temperature, not in just one, but all of them. The icy wet towels covering their backs were having an effect but not as anyone would have predicted. Instead of plummeting, their temperature was rising. Herbert watched in utter astonishment as each of the meditators showed a steady increase in body temperature. Two degrees warmer, then three degrees, then four degrees and still rising.

Benson looked up at the Monks to see steam coming off the wet towels like a boiling kettle. Six degrees increase in skin temperature. Seven degrees and raising further still. Rather than freezing, the Monks were getting hotter!

* * * * * *

With the help of His Holiness the Dalai Lama, in 1981, Dr Herbert Benson and his team of colleagues were permitted unprecedented access to Buddhist Monks in Upper Dharamshala in Tibet.

They witnessed bone chillingly icy wet towels drying on the backs of meditating Monks. The towels were dried by their mastery of mind and physiology during deep meditation and this was measured on quantitative measuring devices. The Monks had complete control of their body purely through focused mental attention and intention.

To say this is extraordinary seems somewhat of an understatement but add this to the fact that Dr Bensons' team also measured a huge decrease in metabolic rate at the same time, would seem to defy what we understand possible from classical science. In other words, although the Monks managed to raise their skin temperature by an astounding 8.3 degree Celsius, their metabolic rate (essentially the rate at which we burn calories to produce heat) dropped by sixty percent.

To put this into some context, whilst we are in a seemingly complete state of 'shut down' during sleep, our metabolic rate will drop between ten and fifteen percent. These Tibetan Monks however, dropped their metabolic rate by sixty percent whilst simultaneously increasing their body temperature.

Conventional understanding would have said this to be impossible because such physiological aspects of body functions are part of the involuntary nervous system and therefore outside of conscious control. However, science evolves with increased knowledge and it is scientists like Dr Benson, who dare to study outside of conventional paradigms, who are the true trailblazers of modern scientific discovery. They are providing us with an undeniable amount of research which opens our minds as to what we humans are truly capable of, what we can achieve, what we can influence and attract into our lives for more health, inner peace and happiness.

Studies show that people who hold a belief in the supernatural or the paranormal are not desperately trying to find meaning to their life because they felt out of control, in fact, such beliefs were positively correlated to an increased sense of control in oneself and life. So, believing that there is a spiritual and supernatural element to life, in which we are inextricably a part of and co-creators of, is not an uneducated view, not a reflection of gullibility or due to a lack of control, in fact, it is quite the opposite.

The belief in something more than the reality we see is increasing whilst the belief in a God-figure is in decline. The National Scientific Foundation report in 2002 shows that population surveys carried out in 1990, 1996 and 2001 demonstrates a steady increase in the belief that humans can influence objects and reality. Today, more than sixty percent of us believe this to be true.

Believing in a reality in which you are the influencer, manifestor and co-creator may seem like gullibility or lack of intelligence to some people and yet, in 2003 the Harris Poll showed an increase in education was correlated with an increase in paranormal beliefs. This survey suggests that the more we know the more we believe that there is something beyond our perceived abilities. Certainly, as highly educated men and women of science delve deeper into the true causation of reality, their minds open to the connection between the reality we experience and our own consciousness.

BELIEVE IT OR NOT

In our current political and social climate, it is hard to know what to believe. Politicians talk the talk during election campaigns but back track on their promises once elected. Laws seem to apply to everyone else but the super wealthy. We are told our troops are sent to fight in foreign lands to protect our nation from weapons of mass destruction which are subsequently never found. Government budget cuts hit the public sectors causing exhausted doctors and nurses to work one hundred-hour weeks and teachers become burnt out whilst city bankers get paid tens of thousands as a Christmas bonus. We are told that members of parliament work to support local people and yet, they are found evading TAX on mass with no arrests. Local authorities spend millions on external cladding for high-rise buildings to make them look aesthetically pleasing to the surrounding wealthier neighbourhoods but apparently, cannot afford to install fire alarms within those flats.

The rich have been getting richer whilst the number of people living in poverty increases. Inequality has risen to the point where one percent of the population holds a net wealth equivalent to ninety nine percent of the population. In other words, a very small amount of people hold the clear majority of the money.

"Instead of an economy that works for the prosperity of all, for future generations, and for the planet, we have instead created an economy for the 1%"

Oxfam Report

Main stream media is owned by billionaires who covertly set the narrative we see, hear and read to support their self-serving agendas. Social media has been infiltrated by those who know how to play on public opinion, so we react to posts and tweets as if they are factual. Conspiracy theorists state that we are duped into playing an elaborate game in which we are unaware participants.

God fearing believers preach answers to life's troubles to be found within a book written when gaps in knowledge were filled with mystical beings and mythology. Depending on which country you are born into or what religious doctrine your parents hold will dictate which God you believe in. Of course, their God is believed to be the correct one because they are told so. Such beliefs create an 'us' and 'them' separation which, when thought through freely, without influence or celestial threat of eternal torture, we can clearly see the madness of theistic religion. According to theistic scripture, if you do not believe in the right God, and the right version of that God, you are marked for everlasting damnation, regardless of your kind, compassionate, loving or altruistic actions on Earth. Equally, of course, you could live a selfish, cruel and harmful life, but will be saved if you repent and believe.

The clever thing about theism is not so much that it has convinced intelligent, and otherwise rational thinking individuals, to believe in an all seeing and judging supernatural entity, but to create absolute fear of challenging that belief. If you dare to think for yourself and challenge such beliefs, you are told how God will punish you.

Religious individuals are told that without Gods moral standards we are nothing more than savage animals, however, with freedom of thought we can recognise the irrationality of such statements. If we are inherently amoral creatures, then how can we know if "the word of God" is moral or immoral? In fact, it is such teachings which themselves create immoral behaviour because they are designed to prevent freedom of thought. For example, if parents learnt that a school teacher has been telling pupils about a ghost which follows each child to monitor their thoughts, behaviours and feelings, parents would be rightly concerned. If parents then found out that the teacher also had the class believe the ghost will torture them for eternity if they misbehave, question the ghosts existence or deviate from what they are told to do, parents would be incensed, and the teacher would surely be dismissed. However, the very same mothers and fathers will not see the parallels between the school ghost and that which is taught to their children in church on a Sunday.

With no grounds to support such illogical and immoral teachings, preachers tell us to hold beliefs based on faith, but faith is not a path to truth.

Of course, a rebuttal from religious followers will be to cite the more moral parables within their chosen book and dismiss those which are immoral. Unwittingly, this is of course an act of freedom of thought and expression of personal moral standards outside of religious teachings.

I understand the need to find higher meaning and purpose to life - and we will talk more about this later - and yet, surely, it is now time for change based on truth, evidence and rational thought enquiry rather than blind faith. Rather than fear-based faith, we should question and examine for ourselves.

Although these political, social, moral and philosophical troubles leave us in a state of distrust, uncertainty or perhaps trepidation, it is important to realise that this critical tipping point has been building for many years. I believe, the fact that we are questioning so much more of what we are told and what we see and hear, will be the catalyst for true and lasting change in humanity. There is a revolution of thought happening and you are a part of it whether you realise it or not.

Prior to this new age of public scepticism, the majority of us followed the 'Pied Piper' and carried out our daily activities with faith. However, for an increasing number of people, this illusory bubble has been wobbling for some time. Questions are now being asked about all aspects of life and alternative avenues of personal growth and development are being rediscovered by many. It is this dubious generation that is causing a shift in awakening. The spreading disbelief in a personified God has not squashed our thirst for a higher spiritual meaning but has triggered bigger prominence for so many of us to find the truth via personal investigation and science.

The historic default has been to insert a God-figure to fill gaps in knowledge to help provide some explanation to the unknown. Nowadays, with scientific advancement and understanding, this 'God of the gaps' reasoning is no longer necessary. The existence of a God is now increasingly recognised as providing no more explanation then that of mythical beasts and supernatural beings created by our distant ancestors to explain a solar eclipse, lightning bolts or shooting stars.

As old and outdated traditions are found lacking in credibility and steadily cast aside, we find ourselves amidst a shift towards personal and spiritual discovery based on science and free thought.

I get the distinct feeling that those in a position of influence and power are increasingly being questioned rather than blindly believed. I firmly believe this is critical to our growth and development as human beings.

Without blind faith, our minds become open to new possibilities and we can think for ourselves freely without judgement or wrath from any fabled authority.

This freedom provides the gift of having an open mind, to peer outside the conformist box. We become free to explore alternative possibilities, listen and learn from scientific research and see how this information fits in with our own logical examination and experiences.

I call upon this inquisitive mind state within you. You, the reader, are discouraged from accepting what I write purely on the basis that it is found in printed ink.

You should question, 'try on' and test the content of this book for yourself. This should be an intellectual investigation by thinking through each concept to test its logical and scientific validity. If something does not sit well, ask questions of it, contemplate it and search internally through your own experiences. This exploration should also be a physical process by way of your own actions and behaviours because, although this book is highly likely to assist positive change towards a more enlightened existence, one fact we know to be certain is the only person who can truly discover the ultimate truth and find blissful spiritual meaning to life, is you. No one else can endow you with enlightenment.

CHAPTER 1

THE ULTIMATE GOAL

On one of my workshops in Cheltenham, United Kingdom, I asked the group what they wanted from life. A straight forward question which elicited blank faces and silence.

On hearing this question, you may identify its importance and yet, have you sat down and answered it yourself?

What is it we really want to gain from life? What is our highest purpose and ultimate goal?

With encouragement the Cheltenham group began pitching answers; what they wanted were values such as security, safety, health, wealth, love, friendships and so forth. As the list exhausted itself I repeated each one by one before asking what would ultimately be gained from the attainment of such values.

Again, I was met with silence until the penny dropped and one student answered "happiness".

The attainment of happiness is the ultimate goal in life. Unbeknown to most, the pursuit of happiness is what motivates everything we do and accomplish everything we want from life. The attainment of happiness is our highest intention and ultimate goal.

Even if we perform actions to benefit others, we do this to aid our own happiness. Making sure our children are clothed, fed, protected and happy means we are happy. Seemingly altruistic acts of kindness are now known to provide the giver with a significant and long-lasting boost in happiness, as measured subjectively via validated questionnaires, and objectively by increases in 'happy hormones' such as oxytocin, dopamine and serotonin.

Happiness supersedes wealth, health and even love. You would not, in your right mind, accept a winning lottery ticket in exchange for your happiness because the money would me nothing if you were miserable. Being healthy and disease free is a key element to our happiness and yet, often health scares and diagnosis of illness cause people to re-evaluate priorities to find a higher state of happiness. People leave relationships despite the gut retching heartbreak because they are not as happy as they believe they can be.

Without recognising it, all our actions, desires and wishes in life are motivated and driven by the desire to attain a higher state of happiness. To attain this ultimate goal of blissful contentment and joy is the true meaning and purpose of life and yet, many of us are oblivious to this fact and are searching in all the wrong places. This is evident from the increasing number of people suffering from depression, in fact, depression now affects three hundred and fifty million people worldwide. The World Health Organisation predicts depression will be the second leading cause of death by 2020 if trends continue.

Records show that signs and symptoms of depression have been consistently rising each decade since the 1960's. Considering our standard of living has also been increasing with each decade, and our lives have become safer and more comfortable in comparison to any previous generation, why is depression on the rise?

SEARCHING OUTSIDE

Researchers in the field of positive psychology have been investigating this linear movement in poor mental health. Four large scale studies have independently traced the point of origin, the point of the 'Big Depression Bang', to the 1960's. Records indicate that before the 1960's symptoms associated with depression such as chronic lethargy, lack of motivation, absence of joy, loss of humour and purpose to life were virtually non-existent. Something must have happened at the end of the second world war causing this new phenomenon to develop in the post war baby boomer generation. The theory which emerged from further research is fascinating.

Professor Martin Seligman, at the University of Pennsylvania, proposes that the issue stems from societies shift towards feeling-good from the collection of materialistic assets.

Seligman's theory fits with the history of the 1950's when Britain and the USA were licking the deep wounds left from the war. To help lift the nations morale and stimulate the economy, there was a concerted government effort to fund and commission films which helped increase the publics drive for success. Depiction of 'Big Screen' characters living opulent lives, attending swanky parties and living seemingly idealistic lives were encouraged, and the nations loved it.

The birth of film ceremonies soon followed, newspaper reporters were encouraged to attend so they could take pictures and publish articles describing the grand events. The actors in attendance reflected their handsome movie characters, arriving in expensive cars, with charming partners wearing fashionable clothing. Soon, entire magazines became dedicated to this new phenomenon of the celebrity. This clever psychosocial and cultural experiment was a success. The public became inspired to desire what they watched and read, causing factories and businesses to bounce back into mass production.

However, there was a significant exchange for this societal change which seems to be our mental health. Prior to the war, life was simple, and happiness was found in hard work, close communities, in family, simple pleasures and social experiences. With the creation of celebrity, the baby boomers of the 1950s were suddenly introduced to a new materialistic world and lives they did not have. As a result, a strong association was made between wealth and happiness. These young impressionable eyes were now exposed to a different, more glamorous world where money and fame seemed to provide the ultimate achievement of happiness.

It is this shift in the direction of external material objects and the focus on attainment of wealth which is thought to be the root cause of the continual rise in depression we see today.

Almost one-third of all teenagers will experience significant symptoms of depression at some point, and by the time they finish secondary school almost fifteen percent will have had a major mental health episode. Perhaps the real catalyst causing this health concern in our children is due to excessive pressure from media and social messages which continue to depict happiness as material success and wealth. In other words, the materialistic message being seen and subliminally regurgitated within the playground, is one that portrays a world of unhappiness without material wealth and possession of 'things'. However, the truth is to the contrary.

In 1976, researchers examined the attitudes of over ten thousand eighteen-year-old students and followed up to measure their life satisfaction eighteen years later. When compared to those who aspired more virtuous achievements the students who sought material wealth, fame and fortune were found to be significantly less happy and satisfied with their lives nearly two decades later. Furthermore, these materialistic adults were found to have higher cases of mental health issues compared to the non-materialists.

But alas, it would seem the cause of the 'Big Depression Bang' is still reverberating through time as magazines, newspapers and celebrity continues to describe materialistic lives as the means to happiness which is having a negative impact on each generation.

A longitudinal study named The American Freshman Survey has been annually recording the attitudes and aspirations of students across America since 1967. At the start of the study, eighty-six percent of students stated that it was very important for them to attain a meaningful life compared to only fifty-two percent in 2005. In contrast, seventy one percent of the 2005 students stated financial wealth as being very important in life whereas only forty-two percent agreed with this in 1967.

When largely focused on the belief that money and 'stuff' is the source of happiness we are ironically setting ourselves up for unhappiness and disappointment. Searching for true and lasting happiness outside of oneself is misguided and misplaced because we adapt to our circumstances and can therefore never find the contentment we expect. Those who expect to find lasting happiness by earning £50,000 discover they are not quite as happy as they anticipated and therefore desire £80,000 instead. Those earning £80,000 do not find the happiness they predicted and therefore desire £100,000 and so forth. We, as a society, are inadvertently driving ourselves further and further away from the ultimate goal we seek.

"I hope everybody could get rich and famous and will have everything they have ever dreamt of, so they will know that it's not the answer"

Jim Carrey

To be clear, money or spending it to attain material belongings is not the cause of unhappiness or indeed the cause of our pending depression epidemic. However, it is the underlying belief that the acquisition of objects and wealth provides us with increased happiness which is the problem. It is this inherent belief which is causing unhappiness rather than material assets themselves.

Therefore, it is of course possible to be excessively affluent and ecstatically happy, but this joy can only be achieved despite this luxurious lifestyle rather than because of it.

After meeting basic human needs such as food, clothing, warmth, security and shelter, we should not believe material possessions provide us with any kind of lasting happiness, satisfaction or contentment.

I am sure you knew this already, but it is vitally important for you to become more conscious of this fact, so you are able to protect yourself from the bombardment of media advertising and social narrative, which will attempt to continue to influence you otherwise.

As you are now fully aware, happiness is the subconscious ultimate goal we are *all* searching for in life, so finding the true source of lasting happiness and discovering how to attain it is the ultimate truth. Everything else we attain outside of this ultimate goal is an added bonus!

Asking what will make you happy is orientated towards the external and what can be gained outside of ourselves to improve our positive emotions. The question we should be asking is *how* can I be happy?

SEARCHING INSIDE

Where our attention goes energy flows and with all our mental attention given to the outside world of materialism, status, success and money, it is no surprise to see mental health and physical health issues continually escalate because we have no energy left for our inner wellbeing and spiritual growth.

We even assign our own internal feelings onto external objects as if those emotions exist within them. We view something outside of ourselves with neural eyes, desire or aversion when no such emotions can be possessed by an object inherently. The expensive car, the grand house or the money in your wallet are inanimate objects which cannot possess happiness or unhappiness. Assigning emotions upon objects is of course an illusion of the mind and we innately understand that an inanimate object cannot possess the emotion we attach to it. Feelings reside within ourselves not outside.

With rational thought, we can also understand that neither can animate objects outside of ourselves - such as another person or animal - possess the emotions we feel towards them. Our emotions and our feelings are integral within our body and do not exist anywhere else outside of it. In this sense, nothing outside of ourselves is truly likeable or dislikeable, it is only perception and interpretation which projects such feelings. It is therefore true to say that an object - whether inanimate or animate - can be perceived to be likeable, dislikeable and neural at the same time depending on who's eyes we are viewing from.

We may say an individual "pushes our buttons" to make us angry, but of course, the ultimate truth is that no one has the power to trigger your emotions aside from yourself. We may say that we dislike an object or even hate a person as if such emotions reside within them, but it is we who bestow such feelings onto the outside world. The truth is that we create our emotions, we chose how to feel, we are masters of the way we feel, and we possess both thoughts and feelings, such qualities cannot exist outside.

When we search inside ourselves we say, "I make me angry" rather than "They make me angry", we say, "That object cannot make me happy or unhappy, only I can create such emotions".

Such internal searching and analytical thought is not only the true path to lasting happiness but also the path to a spiritual awakening and transformation.

This is the journey we shall now take throughout this book.

CHAPTER 2

TWO WORLDS

To successfully take you on this voyage we must first expand knowledge in a layered fashion and take you step by step.

The first thing to appreciate is the fact that the world we see and interact with is not necessarily how it really is. The reality we perceive, by its nature, is a perception and interpretation of the mind.

We are subjected to a salvo of stimuli every waking second. Our eyes take in light and the brain interprets those waves to form the picture we see, our ear drums absorb sound waves and relays the information to our brain for interpretation, and so forth. In fact, it is not just the conventional five senses of sight, hearing, touch, taste and smell which are the bodies sensory antenna, we have twenty-one 'feelers' all taking in information from the external and internal environment.

We have senses for monitoring pressure within our body, we have a built-in thermostat to regulate body temperature, there are senses detecting pain, thirst and hunger. We can feel tension via sensory nodes within muscles, we have sensors to help us determine which way is up and which is down. Proprioceptors provide us with the ability to tell where our body parts are relative to other body parts. Equilibrioceptions provides the ability to keep balanced by sensing body movement in terms of acceleration and directional changes. There are receptors in our lungs, stomach and blood vessels which determine elasticity and chemoreceptors which trigger an area of the medulla in the brain that is involved in detecting blood born hormones.

These senses are constantly and continually monitoring information from the environment and relaying it to the brain. If all that data were to be let through directly, without screening or interpretation, we would be rendered incapacitated and completely dysfunctional.

We have therefore evolved neurological filters, so the brain can cope and process only that which is necessary, important and pertinent at any given time.

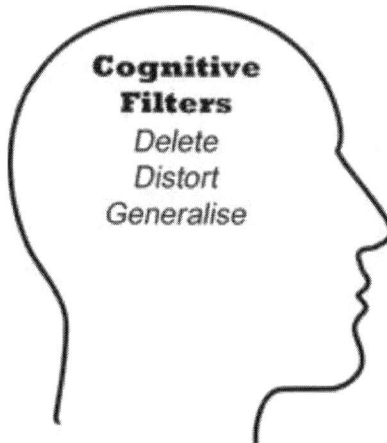

Cognitive Filters
Delete
Distort
Generalise

These filters perform three vital functions:

•   The first is to delete information deemed unimportant or irrelevant at that moment in time. This is the cocktail party example, whereby we can pay attention to the conversation at hand whilst deleting all other external noises around us because they are considered (subconsciously) irrelevant or unimportant in comparison to the discussion we are having. However, if someone were to speak our name somewhere in the room, our filter system highlights that sound as relevant and therefore lets it through for us to become conscious of hearing our name being mentioned.

•   The second function is to distort information to fit in with our beliefs, attitudes and values for example. Perhaps, at some point in this book you may read a scientific fact which does not align with your own beliefs causing you to distort the information to make it more palatable or acceptable to your own belief system. A good example would be the need to resolve cognitive dissonance which can often cause factual information to be distorted to help relieve the discomfort of an internal conflict. An example of this might be a smoker who is fully aware of their habits harmful effects, so to help resolve incongruence between what they know to be true and their behaviour, they may delete and distort the facts to fit with their habit. For instance, they may dismiss some of the health risks by citing those rare people who have smoked all their life and lived to a ripe age. They may also distort some of the risks by stating how little they smoke in comparison to some other people or form a belief that the risks do not apply so much to their low tar cigarettes. Distortion can often be observed in what I call 'Yes But' people. When presented with undeniable facts or irrefutable logic which does not fit in with their world view or belief system, their reply commonly starts with "yes but".

• The third role of these cognitive filters is to generalise information and project the outcome of an event into the future. This is commonly seen in people who have experienced a highly emotional event. Although this one-time event may have happened many years previous and highly unlikely to reoccur, an event perceived to be similar will trigger the belief that they will experience the same outcome as before. Like all filters, this can be limiting or supporting depending whether the original emotion was negative or positive respectively. This is the essence of learned helplessness, whereby a single negative event can negatively influence any future event which is perceived to be similar. The first date which went badly may limit interest in attending any future dates with anyone else. The poorly executed job interview may cause the individual to dismiss any future opportunities. A bad experience on holiday may cause a generalisation about the entire nation. A stressful exam result may form a negative and prevalent view of our abilities and intelligence.

Of course, the filters are not neurological sieves in the physical sense but rather neurological connections or wiring. These filters are therefore neurological networks formed by our past experiences, influenced by cultural background and significant others such as parents, friends and school teachers for example. This results in the formation of our beliefs, attitudes and values and thus, how we view the world. Such memories create our cognitive filters which then influence how the information received by the brain is perceived and interpreted. Language is also a filter because the linguistic meaning, understanding and interpretation of words and sentences will certainly influence our perception of reality.

A nice illustration of the latter is the infamous eyewitness testimony study by Loftus and Palmer (1974). The study involved showing students a short video clip of an accident between two cars after which they were asked to estimate the speed at which the cars were travelling. However, the students were asked in a very specific way with a purposeful choice of words. The students were asked in one of five ways:

About how fast were the cars going when they *smashed* each other?

About how fast were the cars going when they *collided* each other?

About how fast were the cars going when they *bumped* each other?

About how fast were the cars going when they *hit* each other?

About how fast were the cars going when they *contacted* each other?

The results showed that a mere word can have a significant influence on what we perceive to be true. The use of the word 'smashed' created a perception that the cars were travelling around ten miles per hour faster than those students who were asked how fast the cars were going when they "contacted" each other.

A change in a single word can influence what we witness but, of course, because it is our world view, our perception, we believe it to be the truth.

Every man and woman's world picture is and will always remain a construct of their mind and cannot be proven to have any other existence

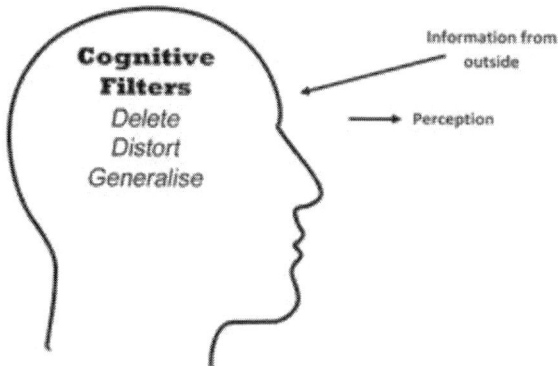

Cognitive Filters
Delete
Distort
Generalise

Information from outside

Perception

These cognitive filters are interconnected and relay information within an instant to form the world we perceive, when, in fact, it is a heavily edited subjective interpretation. The three resultant functions of our cognitive filters are to delete, distort and generalise the information received via our sense from the outside and inside environment to form a world view. Essentially cognitive filters edit reality to provide a personally fabricated view of ourselves and the world outside.

Like a reflection in a mirror, the image is not part of the mirror nor does it exist outside of the mirror. In the same way, the world we perceive is a reflection within our mind.

We can perhaps begin to see the parallels between this and the Buddhist concept of Karma which is the law of cause and effect. The key to understanding Karma is to understand that it is we who cause the effects.

Everything that comes to you is a return of what comes out of you.

CHAPTER 3

A VIRTUAL WORLD OF THE MIND

We can now start to understand that there are two worlds in which we live. The first is true reality, the objective world how it truthfully exists beyond the thoughts and perception of mind. The second is our interpreted mind-version, the subjective world as created by the mind.

Our cognitive filters create a modified and bespoke view of reality and therefore, also influences our thoughts, emotions, behaviours and beliefs too.

Essentially our cognitive filters are neurological networks which are wired within our brain. The only way neurons can wire together is for them to fire together and for this to happen we must have received information from experiences and interactions. Whether it is from our own personal experiences from past events or those vicariously learnt via significant others, our cognitive filters are created by the past and therefore, a direct reflection of our past. Essentially, it is a neurological catalogue of the past in the form of a neurological network. Learning and interpretation of language occurred sometime in our early childhood. Past experiences will have formed beliefs about ourselves, our abilities and capabilities. Values and beliefs will be formed from what we are told by our parents and respected others. Memories of our past are continually referred to each day and we delete, distort and generalise information to conform with this world view.

In this way, the reality we experience today is a reflection of our past. Although each day, hour and moment are brand new, we project our past onto it because that is when and where our neurological networks and subsequent cognitive filters were formed. In other words, we are constantly living in the past. We experience each day with the same mix of deletions, distortions and generalisations which causes the same perceptions, beliefs, attitudes, outlook, thoughts, feelings and behaviours as each day before.

If you thought that the ability to manifest your current and future reality was unbelievable, perhaps now you can begin to see that manifestation is not new to you, you have always been doing it.

We experience very similar patterns of thought because our neural network is wired that way. We therefore experience the same consequential emotions and feelings which in turn create the same set of behaviours.

We know that if we think sad, limiting, upsetting, negative or unhelpful thoughts, they will produce the relevant chemistry within our body to produce the emotional response. Because of the way we feel we react by behaving in a manor appropriate to that emotion. If we feel angry we behave aggressively. If we feel self-doubt we limit our potential. If we feel fearful we avoid that which is thought to be feared. It is a cycle of thought, feeling and behaviour and all of which is a reflection of our past.

This rotation of our past also projects into our future creating a mental concept of what is thought possible and impossible to achieve or attain. Our neural structure may have us believe that it is impossible – or unlikely at best – for us to do or achieve certain things because of our perceived limitations. Our neural wiring sets the scene for our future and we believe that certain things – usually very minor achievements – are possible, whilst other things – usually our ultimate desires and dreams – are impossible fantasies.

This often causes disharmony within us because there is a part of us that settles for the vision of a limited life whilst another part has a desire to attain a much greater ideal life. To resolve this internal conflict, we surrender to the limited life, we convince ourselves that the average level of happiness we are experiencing is okay and assign the ideal vision of our future to a wishful pipe dream.

Of course, most of the people you associate with will be doing the very same thing which reinforces your average existence as the norm. At best, we look around and determine that everyone else seems to have the same issues, worries and struggles to conclude that this is how life is and it is the best we can hope for.

Those who fall outside this mental concept and achieve a higher level of existence are distorted within our mind – because they do not fit with our beliefs and world view - and we differentiate ourselves from them. We say that they are smarter, they have a character trait we do not possess, or they are luckier in some way perhaps.

This restricted reliving of past experiences and associated belief systems means we never attempt to strive towards our ideal life. The most we do is attempt to move away from where we are.

MOVING AWAY FROM

Studies indicate we are increasingly becoming more influenced by media to make us compare ourselves and our lives against those who seem to have more. In fact, when we do this, our self-esteem and image of our life can be damaged. When women are shown images of fashion models it is known to decrease their mood and when men are shown similar pictures they feel less attracted to their wives. Continually presented with what we do not have as something we should have or need to have to be happier is a problem because it causes us to dislike where we are.

Social comparison can not only create disharmony within ourselves and our own lives, it can also cause a social division of "us" and "them". Division is the opposite of inclusion and thus naturally creates rejection. We may feel rejected from a social group because we are different or rejected from a life we perceive to be unattainable. Brain scans show a feeling of rejection lights up areas associated with pain. A sense of rejection is also shown to decrease problem solving abilities, decrease self-regulation, increase depression and aggression. In fact, it is this sense of rejection which is believed to be the root cause of mass killings such as that witnessed in 1999 at Columbine High School. On the other hand, a student survey carried out by Ray Baumeister at Florida State University found that the biggest factor believed to be protecting them from violence is a sense of connection and unity.

When I first graduated from University I secured a job working for the National Health Service. As part of my role I completed interviews and focus groups with residents living in socioeconomically deprived areas. The aim was to find out if there were common themes impacting their wellbeing. It quickly became apparent that many of the residents saw their homes as a safe ground and everything outside of their front door was not their responsibility. Old mattresses, rubbish and unwanted furniture was dumped in the streets making it unsightly and unpleasant to walk around. Adults blamed the younger residents for the issues and the elderly residents were frightened of the gangs of youths hanging around on the streets so rarely ventured outside. Then, when I interviewed the young people who formed such gangs, the common theme was a lack of community and subsequent sense of rejection. The adults held an 'each man for himself' mentality and the youngsters formed their own communities in the form of a gang. I recall one young man saying, "No one cares about us, so why should we care about them". Everyone in this area wanted to *move away* from their current situation rather than *towards* a unified solution.

It struck me how this mindset was a self-creating and self-supporting social system. The "us" and "them" mentality fed into the situation, further driving them apart and reducing their own wellbeing. However, it can be hard to prevent comparison between ourselves and others, but this is the root cause of discontentment and the desire to move away from it.

There is a fundamental and profound difference between moving towards an ideal vision of our future and moving away from our current position. The former has thoughts, energy and emotions set towards the future whilst the latter directs thoughts, energy and emotions onto where we already are.

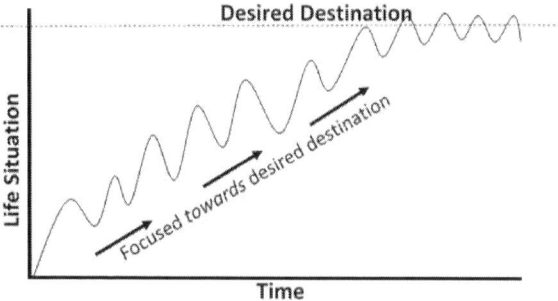

Having a destination towards which we are directing our focus and energy drives our behaviours and life onwards, and if we remain dedicated to this vision, we will continue to move in this direction until we accomplish it. Once at the desired destination our motivation may dip but our neurology will be rewired and set to keep driving us forwards once again.

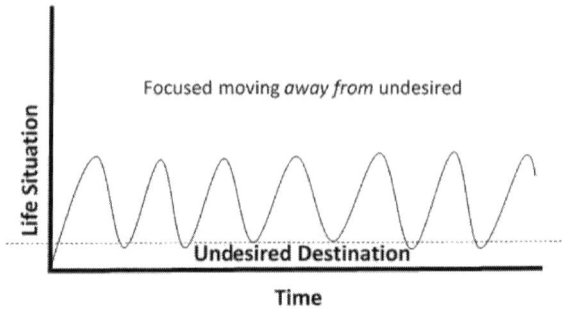

Focused moving *away from* undesired

Life Situation

Undesired Destination

Time

Conversely, with an 'away from' mindset, we are initially motivated to take action and improve our situation but as we gain distance away from the negative situation, and the associated thoughts and feelings dissipate, we feel better and as if we have achieved our goal. Now we are no longer driven to continue and thus, fall back to the same or similar situation and thus, the cycle of moving away from what we do not want starts again.

Once again, do you see the same cycle of reliving the past as it continues to play out in our future. It is the same world view repeating which in turn reinforces our cognitive filters and the perception of what is possible and impossible.

The difference between these two neural networks is that one is designed to move us towards what we want whilst the other is dedicated to moving away from what we do not want.

The mental focus and energy applied to what we do not want cultivates a significant problem because; what you focus on grows and what grows in abundance you see in abundance.

By focusing on what you do not want to manifest you will train your mind to seek out the very thing you wish to move away from. Just like you can learn a new language for example, by reciting and revisiting what you have learnt, the more you comprehend and hear. Similarly, by practicing negative emotions such as worry, anger, stress or envy through mental attention and focus, we literally condition the mind to seek them out and, what we seek, sure enough, we will find.

Facebook is a perfect model of this cognitive system. The algorithm used by Facebook works to show more of what you have paid attention to. Whether it is watching videos, clicking 'like' on certain content, commenting on posts or sharing them, the more you engage with a specific theme or nature of content, the more Facebook will present it to you.

Recently I had to go into a hardware store to pick up some paint brushes. As it was a quick chore my wife decided to wait in the car. I was gone no more than five-minutes but when I returned to the car Helen was in floods of tears.

It transpired that she had watched a video via Facebook on her phone. The video was of a dog being beaten which was obviously distressing, especially to a compassionate and caring sole such as my wife. She is an advocate for animal welfare so naturally followed pages on Facebook which share her views. One day a picture pops up on her Facebook feed showing a malnourished and sorry looking dog in a cage. The accompanying caption read: "Share if you are against animal cruelty", so she shares the picture. This interaction and focus on a negative image was logged within Facebook software which responded by presenting her with similar pictures which, in turn, she pays attention to and interacts with. Noting this trend in Helens' behaviour, Facebook shows more upsetting images. Outraged and upset by such pictures and videos Helen engaged with these posts via comments, angry-face emojis and shares it for others to see. This mental attention reinforces the connection between her profile and animal cruelty rather than animal welfare. Soon, her page is awash with images of animals being mistreated and even killed. Continually being presented with disturbing pictures in favour of positive images, she forms a distressing view of a world in which people are cruel, unkind and repulsive.

Through her tears Helen said to me, "Why are people so horrible?". This is a generalised statement because what she had unwittingly created was a view of a world full of heinous human behaviour. Due to what she had been paying more attention to on Facebook, the positive information about animals being cared for was gradually deleted and what she was presented with on her feed was a distorted picture of reality biased towards cruelty. Thus, her mind formed a corresponding view of humans through generalisation forming a universal view of "people" being unkind.

The Facebook algorithm is virtually identical to our own cognitive filter system. The more we focus on what is not right with our lives, what we do not want for ourselves or within the world in general, the more we pay attention to it and thus, we wire our neural connections to become highly tuned into finding and seeing that which we wish to avoid. We end up deleting the good things in favour for that which we do not wish to see. We also distort any good information and generalise to form a negative belief and perception about the world and life.

For example, a person who is obsessively focused on avoiding illness may develop anxiety about death and disease. As a result, their mind becomes filled with worry and fear, they over exercise and become malnourished, making life less enjoyable, exhausting, more stressful and their immune system becomes compromised causing them to become ill.

What we focus on grows within the mind

In evolutionary terms, most of us will have a natural cognitive bias towards negative thoughts because such thoughts would have helped keep our prehistoric ancestors alive. In a world where man was the hunted as well as the hunter, just walking outside the cave dwelling was a life-threatening situation and therefore having an overly cautious, sceptical and fearful mindstate would have been an advantage. However, in modern-day life, we have no such things to worry about and yet, we maintain this "Be fearful", "Be distrusting" "Be cautious" mindset.

Due to the way our modern minds have been educated by a media saturated culture which rarely shows the kindness and love within the world, our mental focus is largely directed onto what we do not want.

- I don't want to feel unsafe

- I don't want to go to Hell

- I don't want to be financially poor

- I don't want to get sick

- I don't want a loveless relationship

- I don't want to fail

- I don't want to be stressed

With a mind being programmed by fear and social separation via negative news, fearmongering media and mass advertising showing what we do not have, we are literally being programmed to move away from where we currently are. So, we work harder to earn more money, we may change jobs or change our relationship status, we may move to a new house or country or we buy more possessions. We have not moved towards our ideal destination, all we have done is move a small distance from where we were. However, each time we take a step away from where we are we feel better and so our motivation to continue stops. Once again, this new destination is not our ideal life and ultimate goal, it is just a step or two away from where we were, so eventually, we end up back in the same situation and the cycle of wanting to move away from our current life starts again.

Imagine you are at the bottom of a pit where the ground is filled with mud and filth. Motivated to get out of this pit and away from the sodden foul-smelling floor you climb the cliff face. As you climb you begin to find drier more solid ground and the stench from the pit begins to diminish. At this point you are satisfied to be far enough away from the bottom and stop climbing. You have not reach the top of course, where all manner of wonders and better opportunities may lie, but you have achieved your goal to be away from where you were. Many people perch themselves onto the side of the pit for the rest of their lives believing this position is as good as life gets. For others, when life gets tough and the rain comes, they slide back down.

Understandably, when financially deprived our mental attention is highly tuned into and attached to your current state of poverty creating a desire to move away from the situation. However, a mind trained to focus on the fear of being poor is motivated to move away from the feeling rather than toward attaining financially security. Thus, when we have a little more money in our bank account we feel more relaxed and stop striving forwards which eventually leads to the gradual decline back to strict fiscal measures once again. Of course, when noticeably close to poverty again the motivation to move away from it increases once again and the cycle continues. Yet, another repetition of our past.

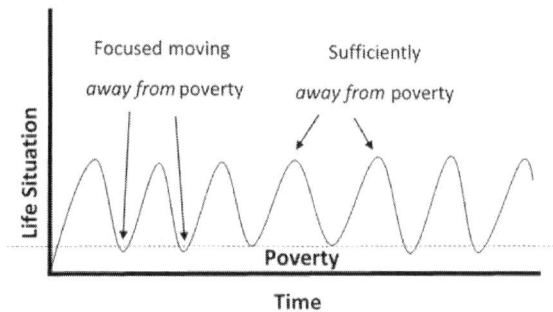

Subjecting yourself to a diet to lose weight is another prime example. Eating healthily and taking up regular physical activity is the only way to lose weight safely and maintain that weight for life whereas diets are focused on unhelpful, often miserable eating plans which are unrealistic in the long-term. However, those keen to move away from being overweight, rather than towards a healthier lifestyle, will take up such diets and lose weight rapidly. Once far enough away from their unwanted weight they fall back into old feeding habits (especially because the diet is unsustainable) and typically end up with a lower metabolism, less health, less fitness and higher body mass than before. And so, the yo-yo starts again as they continue to relive their past.

In other words, when attention is largely given to what you want to avoid you will repeatedly return to what you least desire. This can be a common cycle in many areas of life and will negatively impact confidence and self-esteem unless it is broken.

For instance, often we mentally list and remind ourselves of all the things we no longer want to experience in life and are therefore highly tuned into them. So, to move away from such unpleasantness, we adjust a few things, change routines, change circumstances somewhat, to create distance away from what we want to remove from our lives. However, as soon as these adjustments give us the slightest bit of respite, we have achieved our goal (i.e. to simply move away from where we were) and therefore motivation to make permanent changes weakens rapidly. Thus, we end up back where we do not want to be.

The most self-evident of this cyclical attraction is noticed when we desire to get away from stress. When noticeably being affected by stress we make positive changes by eating more nutritious food, cutting down on caffeine, take actions to relax, cut down on alcohol and take up physical activity perhaps. Naturally, these actions make us feel better, we gain more energy, mental clarity and resilience which helps us cope with daily demands. At this point our motivation to continue with these positive lifestyle changes dwindles because as soon as we start to feel less strained we have achieved the goal of moving away from stress. Before long we are back where we started, eating sugary food to give us energy which in turn causes blood sugar crashes throughout the day. To pick us up we drink more coffee which decrease clarity of mind and disturbs our sleep. Feeling exhausted we stop exercising and start drinking alcohol in the evenings to depress the mind. Mentally and physically tired we are less able to cope, and stress becomes a part of life again as we relive our past once again.

MOVING TOWARDS

Now imagine you are in the same pit previously described. You look up at the cliff face, right up as far as you can see and decide that you will not stop until you have reached the very top. Now you are motivated to move towards the cliff top, to leave the pit completely. Your mind is not focused on moving away from the bottom but dedicated to reach its highest point. With this frame of mind, you may rest when weary and tired, but you are not settled because you have not reached your goal yet. You remain looking up, persistently and intently focused towards your desire and, if at times you slip a short way, you gather your footing and refocus towards your destination every time.

With practice you can train your mind to shift perspective and focus towards what you do want.

- I don't want to feel unsafe becomes *you will be safe*
- I don't want to go to Hell becomes *you will live an honest and kind life*

- I don't want to be financially poor becomes *you will be financially secure*
- I don't want to get sick becomes *you will be healthy*
- I don't want a relationship lacking in love becomes *you will have a relationship full of love*
- I don't want to fail becomes *you will succeed*
- I don't want to feel stressed becomes *you will feel peace*

This subtle but significant shift in mental attention onto what you *do* want to manifest in your life will cause you to continue forwards and upwards without regression. With a switch in mental focal point you break the repetition of past experiences and you enter a new life rather than repeating the same old life.

At first glance it may seem as though a mind focused on getting away from what you wish to avoid is synonymous with a mind focused on moving towards what you wish for. In a sense they are similar because both have the power to manifest and attract but the critical difference is that 'towards-minds' create permanent changes whilst 'away-minds' create temporary change. A towards mindset is never far away from what you want whilst an 'away from' mind is never far from the very thing you do not want. Having an 'away from' mindset repeatedly brings you back to what you least want whilst a 'towards' mindset repeatedly drives you towards what you do want.

If you are continually looking to achieve inner peace and the ability to cope, you will continually find ways to achieve that desire and rewire your mind correspondingly making it habitual and easy to find. Conversely, if you are always looking at how stressed, difficult and harsh your life and the world is, you will continually find stress and difficulty. This is like a spotlight scanning for thoughts and situations to find and confirm our view of the world. Also, with an 'away from' mindset your subconscious is set to simply create distance between you and what you do not want in your life rather than continually performing actions that are aligned to achieve what you want.

The key issue to reflect on is the fact this cycle has been playing out, and will continue to play again and again unless your neural network is changed to cause change in thoughts, feelings and behaviours. This book will help you accomplish this.

WHAT IS IT YOU REALLY WANT?

Because we are unconsciously programmed with an away-mindset, rarely do we turn around to see what it is we want. Using the pit analogy once more, rather than looking down at the bottom of the pit we need to turn around and focus on the top.

When I ask students on my workshops what it is they want from life, I can see their minds thinking about their current life and what is lacking from it. Never have I heard a student make a clear, definitive, confident and well thought through statement about what they want from life. It is always a sporadic and largely spontaneous list of external qualities and elements of things they do not currently have in life. For instance, after some degree of thought students will list things such as, more financial security, to be healthier, to be happier, to have more time with family, to have more freedom, to have more leisure time or to have a better job. These students are looking to move away from because all statements allude to a lacking in something.

No one has ever made a visionary statement such as:

To wake every morning and feel heart felt gratitude for my life as I marvel at the many gifts I have within it. To feel the soft cotton sheets against my skin as the sun shines through the window bringing with it the joyous morning chorus of the birds outside. My face and heart will smile as I feel love for my life.

If someone said such a thing on my workshops I would applaud. It would be clear that the individual has truly thought about what they really want, how it would feel and what they would gain. This would be evident to me by the poetic description which paints the picture, a picture that they have clearly within their mind. They are looking *towards*.

When we go on holiday most people are very organised. Potential destinations are thoroughly researched, we may ask a travel agent for information and advice, we may even ask friends who have visited places before. We investigate costs, flight availability and accommodation until we have it all planned out. With each element of our holiday thought through as much as possible our travels are likely to go smoothly and we arrive at our destination with ease.

Rarely do we pay such meticulous attention to our own lives and where we wish to be. We plod along with an ambiguous idea of how we would like our lives to improve based on the issues we are currently facing but seldom do we take the time to be absolutely clear on our desired destination.

So, the first step is to take time to think about what you want. What it would look like, what it would feel like, what you would smell, what you would be touching and be able to do. Develop a clear and concise image in your mind. Imagine what it would feel like, see how you look and behave. Make this image as real as possible within your minds-eye so your body feels how you would feel once at this destination.

If you fail to do this, you will drift along reliving your past and never arrive anywhere different from where you currently are.

CHAPTER 4

CAUSALITY AND CONTROL

Having the motivation to change anything in your life must begin with a sense of having personal control. In fact, autonomy and high motivation go together.

Psychologists talk about Locus of control. Individuals who view life challenges as being within their control will adapt, make positive choices and adjust their own behaviours to overcome hurdles. In contrast, people who have a bias towards an external locus of control, and therefore see many of life's trials as being outside of their own influence, will do little to change and overcome them.

As part of my postgraduate research I studied the beliefs held by cardiac patients to see if these had an impact on their health behaviours and risk of future coronary event. Perhaps somewhat unsurprisingly, those who believed their heart attack was due to external causes such as fate, genetics or work for example, would do little to take control their future health and subsequently were at higher risk of another heart attack. Conversely, patients who believed their future health was within their own control would take up more physical activity, modify eating habits, quit smoking and reduce alcohol. Because these patients believed they were in control, their risk of further ill health significantly reduced and their overall quality of life improved.

Studies show that people with a predisposition towards internal locus of control (i.e. control is within their power) are more optimistic, healthier, less depressed, less stressed and more resilient. People who believe they are masters of their lives and future, recover faster from injury and are more likely to seek help when needed.

In comparison, those with an external locus of control will tend to suffer more, are prone to depression and have lower self-esteem. A study carried out by Michael Marmot at the University of London showed that workers with the least sense of control were twice as likely to have a heart attack when compared with employees with the highest sense of personal control.

In fact, the three things we all want is a sense of having more control of ourselves and our lives, having more time and having more self-efficacy and all three are interconnected.

Without control, life is a gauntlet of uncertainty and our own ability to be able to achieve our wishes and desires are seldom realised or attempted.

To achieve anything in life, we first must hold a belief that it is possible and such a belief is founded on our degree of self-efficacy.

Self-efficacy is the confidence we have about our own ability to control and manipulate our environment and to successfully navigate past hurdles and challenges. No matter how much we desire to attain an outcome in our life, any belief gaps about our own capabilities can destroy self-confidence. Experiments by Professor Albert Bandura and his colleagues consistently showed that self-belief to be a far greater predictor of success than academic status, ability or intelligence.

For you to achieve your desires and accomplish your deepest wishes therefore, you must first, and above all, believe that you can achieve them and by association, you have the ability to control and direct your life to arrive at your desired destination.

Look back over your life so far and write down all the things that you have achieved. No matter how great or small. Write down your successes at school, your sporting achievements perhaps, successful interviews, relationships and all the things you have successfully changed to better your life. Think about all those times when things did not quite go to plan, but you pulled through. Think about all those times when you were the support for a friend or family member in need. Think about the things you have wished for and successfully attained. Once you have done this you will recognise how much of your wishes have come true and how you were the cause of them.

Typically, we perceive ourselves as having little control in life because we are attempting to stabilize the unstable, to make permanent the impermanent and to grasp at that which is perpetually changing. This is the root cause of all our worldly problems. All of second world reality is in a continuous state of change. The environment changes in temperature from one moment to the next. Objects rot and colours fade with time. Our bodies are constantly changing inside and outside. When happy we attempt to maintain the situation, but it will of course change, so we attempt to recreate the past or wish to be somewhere else. Each second is never the same as the next and yet, we attempt to prevent this natural way of things because we are focused outside rather than inside.

Our problems come in the form of worries and stressors from the persistent fight against the hassles which are perceived as the cause. Often, without consciously being aware of it, many of us feel like life is something that happens to us rather than us being something that happens to life.

People will say this is just the way life is which of course is correct if they believe this to be true. With such a belief, there is no intention to make changes, no motivation and no effort applied. We battle onwards through life, which is often seen as something to wrestle with and to fight against. With this perception, many of us are swept along by life without begin consciously engaged with it. Seldom do we stop and pay attention to the interactions and influences between our thoughts, feelings and behaviours. Without noticing these interconnected actions and reactions between us and the world, we never truly get to study and understand how to enhance our lives and transcend the troubles and sufferings. Days, weeks, months and years become reduced to a list of chores to organise, tasks to manage and difficulties to pacify rather than a planned and controlled journey towards a desired destination.

The important thing to recognise about the amount of control we have regarding an issue is the belief held about our ability to change it. To obtain a staunch belief about our ability to change our future and take control of it, we first must know the cause of that which we wish to change. For instance, if we have a pain in our foot we must identify the cause of this discomfort, so we may be relieved from it.

Just like we feel the need to control uncomfortable emotional dis-ease such as anger, stress, hatred and sadness, there is an underlying need for patients to feel in control of their disease too.

It would also seem that the severity of a health event such as a heart attack is mistakenly linked to recovery time and because patients need to have a sense of control over their condition, there is a linear relationship between a patients perceived severity of condition with their feelings of vulnerability. In other words, the longer a person feels emotionally or physically unwell, the more severe they think their problem is and therefore will feel fearful and vulnerable as a result. Furthermore, because feeling afraid and vulnerable is deeply unpleasant these people also have a heightened need to control their illness to relieve the fear and anxiety. However, to control something which is making you unwell, you first need to know what the cause of your suffering is.

Of course, in the case of cardiac patients one could say that the cause of their distress is the fact that they have experienced a heart attack, but this is not the cause of their condition. Similarly, we could say that the cause of our stress, dissatisfaction with life and struggles are the external elements and yet, these are not the cause of our feelings. For example, we could say that the busy traffic caused our stress. But where is the cause exactly? In which car precisely does your stress reside or is it found within all cars collectively? In the same way we may say our faulty computer caused us to feel anger, but the computer does not infect us with anger like a mosquito with malaria. On certain days we may say that our children cause us worry and yet, on other days we say they cause us so much joy. How can our children possess feelings of joy and unhappiness at the same time?

To effectively manage or control the stressors, problems, worries and dis-ease, first you must establish a cause, which can then lead to appropriate changes to eradicate the problem. This makes common sense when you compare it to something like a leaky water pipe in your house. To rectify the problem of water coming through the ceiling, first you need to know what is causing your unwanted water feature.

Commonly we assign the unpleasant emotions onto objects outside of ourselves and cite them as the cause. We may recognise that we feel stressed, angry or upset, but we focus entirely on the feeling rather than what is truthfully causing the feeling. Often, we simply state that it is just the way life is. Life is a struggle and that is that.

From my research, I identified a link between severity of dis-ease and cause. For example, the more stressed we feel the more we attribute the cause as being something outside of ourselves and therefore outside of our control. In other words, if in a normal situation we would see a particular life challenge as controllable, when we are acutely anxious we re-evaluate the cause as being uncontrollable and assign blame onto other people or things outside of our self. Interestingly, research suggests that males have a higher tendency to see their own actions or thoughts as the cause of their situation whereas females tend to blame family, partners or such things as their personality.

If we believe the cause of our disharmony to be uncontrollable then of course, by definition, we do not attempt to control it.

Again, this psychological issue is found in hospital patients too and has repercussions to their health. Patients who believe the cause of their condition is uncontrollable, will make fewer lifestyle changes and therefore show a poorer physical recovery as a result. Of course, this then becomes a self-fulfilling prophecy, whereby they feel unwell for longer which increases the belief that their condition is more severe, and the cause is outside of personal control.

We experience a problem and blame the cause onto people or circumstances. In this way we view the unpleasant feelings as something separate from ourselves, detached from our actions and therefore uncontrollable. Thus, we justify our feelings with no attempt to change it because the cause is believed to be outside not inside. The truth however is different.

The external event, situation, people or problem is not the cause of negative feelings because emotions do not exist within external objects. Although you may understand this intellectually, I encourage you to take time and examine this fact deeply. No matter how hard it may be to believe at this moment in time, the fact is, you cause your own emotions, you control your own emotions and therefore you can change them.

To say we cannot help the way we feel is to surrender control. We can, and frequently do, change our internal state. If this were not true, then how is it that we can find being stuck in traffic a pleasant opportunity to take time out and relax whilst other times we get intensely stressed, frustrated or even angry? Equally, if the cause of our emotional – and by association our physical discontentment - did not reside within our own mind then how can we feel love for someone one minute and anger toward them the next?

The cause of dis-ease and suffering lies within the mind

Nothing can cause you to get upset apart from you. Your mind 'pushes your buttons' and no one else has this control.

The control of dis-ease and suffering lies within the mind

In the same situation you may find it pleasant on one occasion and unpleasant on another. How can this be if your mind were not the cause?

The ability to make permanent and profound changes therefore resides in mastering control of your mind.

There is a story about an enlightened man who was teaching at a village gathering. An angry passer-by stopped to listen to the Buddha.

"Who are you to teach such things?" said the onlooker aggressively.

"I am no one" replied the Buddha.

"You people make me angry with your preaching and witchcraft" Said the man.

In a calm and peaceful manner, the Buddha asked: *"When friends visit your home, do you feed them?"*

Slightly taken aback with the question the man pauses before answering, *"Yes, I provide food for them to eat"*

To which the Buddha continued, *"And if they do not eat the food you have provided, to whom does that food belong?"*

"The food is all mine of course" replies the man maintaining his aggressive tone.

With a gentle voice the Buddha replies, *"The same is true with regard to your anger. You created it and, although you offer it to me I do not wish to take it. Regarding your anger, who is not aggressive? Regarding insults, who is not insulting? That with which you have taunted me, who is not taunting? It is yours sir, it is all yours"*

Obviously, if the traffic is bad, the car breaks down or the kids play up, there is not much we could have done to control it but whether that situation becomes pleasant, unpleasant or neutral is entirely dependent on our ability to control our mind. As we know from experience, negative emotional states are always accompanied with additional physical and psychological problems so, by failing to address the cause of all our problems (our mind) we ignorantly add additional problems to life's challenges.

For example, a flat tyre on the way to work is a problem but if we attribute our resultant stress, frustration or anger onto the flat tyre, we will never attempt to reduce the negative feelings or physical strain added. If we become stressed about the situation, our heart rate and blood pressure increase, muscular tension increases, creative thinking and coping abilities are significantly reduced and thus, we now have additional problems.

With clarity of understanding you can recognise the cause of dis-ease as the mind. With the cause identified, steps can be taken to take back control and make significant and profound changes.

People with a sense of self-mastery and control of life have both physical and psychological higher states of wellbeing compared to those with less awareness of control.

How do you master your mind and prevent yourself from spending the rest of your life chasing that which cannot be caught? How do you master your mind to be free from negative emotions? How do you master your mind so that it becomes firmly devoted to move towards the ultimate goal of peace and happiness?

The first thing to do is contemplate four truths about your life:

Truth One: Second world reality naturally changes with time. No second is the same as the next. No object will be the same today as it is tomorrow.

Truth two: The root cause of human stress and emotional suffering is the attempt to control these normal life changes which exist outside of oneself.

Truth three: The realisation that we have control via our own mind. Mastery of oneself is where freedom from cyclical unhealthy or unwanted behaviours can be found.

Truth four: Self-mastery comes by following these eight steps:

    i.   Understanding: Study yourself and your mind so you can understand your ability to change and control the external via searching internally.

    ii.   Intention: Commit to attaining self-mastery and be in control of yourself and your future.

    iii.   Speech: Control what you say to help control the way you think, feel and behave.

iv. Action: Control what you do. Behave peacefully and harmoniously to support your health and wellbeing.

v. Livelihood: Avoiding making a living in ways that cause physical or emotional harm.

vi. Effort: Apply effort to cultivate positive states of mind and body.

vii. Mindfulness: Spend time developing awareness of mind and body rather than being led by your emotions.

viii. Concentration: Practice concentrating through meditation to develop the mental focus necessary for mindful awareness.

It is these eight steps to self-mastery and control which we will now encompass within this book.

CHAPTER 5

UNDERSTANDING

Often, the power which lies within our own abilities to change our future goes unrecognised because we attach ourselves within the problem. Imagine walking inside a maze and it is hard to find your way out. Now imagine the same scenario but this time you have a map which enables you to view from outside the maze. The same applies for your own life. Because it is your life and your experiences are within it, it can be hard to 'step out' and view it from another perspective.

Have you ever had a problem which you have struggled to find a solution to? Perhaps it was a puzzle, something you were attempting to fix or a problem you could not solve at work? But then a friend comes along and quickly points out ways in which to resolve your situation. You may have spent hours or perhaps days trying to make progress and all it took was another persons' outside view point to navigate you.

Equally, have you been that 'outside' person? Have you helped a friend overcome a hurdle in their life by pointing the possible routes out of their situation which they could not see? You could see the possible solutions to your friends' issue because you are outside of the problem looking in. The answers you provide are often simple and obvious to you but for the individual within the issue, such pathways out are hard to see because they are attached within the problem.

Even when resolutions to a problem are pointed out to us, we frequently dismiss them as if the problem is too great to overcome, like we are fixed to the problem as if it holds us prisoner.

The first understanding is to recognise that problems have no boundaries, they do not possess the ability to attach you or your emotion to it. If you feel encased within a problem or situation which you are struggling to get free from, you should expand awareness to push the psychological boundaries to break free and this book aims to help you do this.

UNDERSTANDING FEELINGS

It seems impossible for us to experience a person, situation or object without feelings. We see something or experience an event which triggers either a pleasant feeling, unpleasant feeling or neutral feeling. Whether awake or asleep, our mind has us believe that the feelings are caused by the object or situation. In other words, the objects and experiences we have in our waking states and dream states are alleged to possess pleasant, unpleasant or natural feelings.

For example, we may see a person whom we dislike and say that they are unpleasant and yet, the very same person could be seen as pleasant by someone else. We may find a certain type of food unpleasant, but another person will happily eat that food with pleasure.

Beauty, they say, is in the eye of the beholder or more accurately, beauty is in the mind of the beholder. In the Western world our minds are conditioned to see a person's particular physical features, stature and fashion as neutral, pleasant or unpleasant, whereas, certain African tribes will see beauty in a completely different way. Neither view is false or incorrect, and in fact, the feelings evoked are very real in either case. What one person sees as beautiful or pleasant, ugly or unpleasant entirely depends upon the mind.

Objects and circumstances are viewed as having pleasant, unpleasant or neutral qualities which are perceived to be separate from ourselves. We believe that the object holds these feelings when it is not the characteristics of the object but rather the characteristics of our own mind. Feelings are existent only in our mind and not inherent within an object and therefore no object or situation can be said to be pleasant or unpleasant.

For me, the strangest thing about any emotion is its presence in the first place. What is a feeling exactly? Where do they come from? We feel it within our body, but its exact location cannot be pinpointed. Often the location and description of the sensation differs between one person and the next. The intensity of the feeling can alter too, and this can completely change how we would describe it and its locality within the body. For some people it moves and for other people it is static. Some say it has weight, density or pressure. I have had clients describe certain feelings as a knot or a ball, I have even heard clients give the feeling of stress heat which radiates or pulsates.

Due to this nature of mind, we perceive objects as unpleasant, pleasant or neutral and we attach the relevant feelings onto those objects. However, it is not the object which holds the feeling, but the perception cultivated within the mind.

As a result, we activity seek out more of the objects our mind views as pleasant whilst avoiding those which are unpleasant or neutral, a process which causes us to discriminate against certain things in favour of others.

The problem to all life's woes is this combination of attachment of feelings onto objects and resultant discrimination. Nowadays, we have attached pleasant feelings onto objects which are unimportant in the grand scheme of things and therefore, our mind is focused on the attainment of these objects at the expense of those which should be seen as more important.

It is this type of misplaced attachment and discrimination which cause us to feel jealousy, hatred, anger and stress for example.

UNDERSTANDING NON-ATTACHMENT

Let's say you wake up on a Monday morning instantly dreading the day ahead, your mind jumps from the work load in your job, the chores at home, your money worries, concerns for family and the future. You notice how stressed this makes you feel. You notice this feeling more and more as you take deep breaths to catch your breath and subdue the feeling building within your chest. As you continue to notice how you feel, the more unhelpful thoughts will manifest within your mind, which increases the intensity of negative emotions. Now you are feeling anxious and become short-tempered. With mental dedication onto how you are feeling, the negative thoughts flow freely and you become locked into a self-perpetuating cycle as your worrying thoughts continue to feed your emotions and vice versa.

You may have experienced something similar and we know that thoughts direct our mental attention which in turn creates a feeling. As our mind becomes locked onto and attached to an object, sensation or event, the stronger this attachment gets and the harder it is to mentally, physically and emotionally let go.

Similarly, if we believe money or possessions to be the source of happiness we will become attached to what we have and that which we desire to have. Just as with the thought-feeling-behaviour cycle, this will create a cycle of unending discontentment as we will never be truly satisfied.

A wise person will recognise this process and work to release themselves from such attachment. To practice non-attachment, it is not necessary or possible to avoid all objects of attachment. Rather than trying to avoid them by heading off to a cave or isolating yourself, successful non-attachment can be achieved by recognising the faults of the mind and then take effort to let go.

Because we live in a rapacious world in which we are subjected to a barrage of messages from media, marketing and advertisements, the biggest attachment we have nowadays is desirous attachment to objects. We desire to hold tightly, both psychologically and physically, onto the objects we have had in the past, objects we have now and objects we do not have.

The three divisions of desirous attachment are therefore:

1.   Desirous attachment to past objects

2.   Desirous attachment to present objects

3.   Desirous attachment to future objects

To be clear, desire in and of itself is not necessarily a limiting attribute towards happiness and personal growth. For example, you are perhaps reading this book with the desire to attain spiritual development which is a virtuous desire and will lead you along the path to the ultimate goal of happiness for yourself and others.   The issue exists with non-virtuous attachment to the world outside.

1. DESIROUS ATTACHMENT TO PAST OBJECTS

Whether it is people, physical objects or events we once had or experienced, to mentally and emotionally hold onto such things is to cause us suffering and limit personal and spiritual progress. These things are gone and no longer exist but with desire still attached we struggle to move on and we remain, both emotionally and psychologically, in a place which is non-existent. I.e. the past. This can not only cause us emotional suffering but moreover, keep us stuck in a world where the ultimate goal of lasting happiness cannot be found. With a mind stuck in an external world how can we expect to find the truth of reality which can only be discovered within the internal world?

Letting go of attachment to past events or people does not mean to forget or stop loving but it does mean we can be free to move on and engage in today with more wonder and enjoyment. Love is a virtuous mind that creates only peace and happiness, whereas attachment is never virtuous and causes pain and problems.

Equally, with a desirous mind firmly attached to the past, how can we expect to find the ultimate goal and ultimate truth which can only be found within the here and now?

2. DESIROUS ATTACHMENT TO PRESENT OBJECTS

The more we direct and focus our mental attention onto external objects the more attached we become to them and this is an increasing issue in Western society. We are so mentally wrapped onto 'things' outside of ourselves that we end up mentally attached to them and this is where all our efforts and energy is directed. Of course, this process is largely subconscious, and we are mostly unaware that we are attached to the outside world of 'things', materials, objects, people and, of course, money.

This attachment causes issues because when we lose what we have we suffer emotionally, like a child being taken from their mother or father. We covert the objects within our possession and our desires are attached to that which we do not have. This process of mental and emotional attachment, caused by dedication of thought onto objects outside of oneself, will cause more unhappiness. Besides, with all our energy directed outside, how much energy do we have left for ourselves inside?

Whether it is due to the end of our life or the natural entropy of things, all things outside of our self will change and come to an end. No matter how much we may dislike the thought, nothing outside our self is permanent and we cannot force this to be otherwise. We should therefore, avoid becoming attached to anything non-virtuous because attachment to objects, possessions or people will ultimately cause more problems and sadness.

This may not sit well with you at first but let me clarify.

We can understand that coveting material possessions and metaphysically attaching ourselves to them is neither helpful or healthy. When we hold tightly onto our possessions we wish for them to always remain unchanged, but of course, all second world things are impermanent and therefore our grasping is folly. You could say that your designer bag makes you happy or your favourite shoes provides you with joy. However, if you rely on such things as a source of lasting happiness you will become disappointed because these objects wear away and change with time, and thus, leaving you looking for something else outside of yourself to fill your happiness void once again.

Holding strong attachment to objects is to believe that we own it, we control it, it belongs to us and us alone. Such attachment is not only an illusion of mind (as you shall discover later) and a barrier to spiritual development, it can also lead to possessiveness, selfishness, jealousy and unkind actions. We can likewise understand that our material assets do not mean anything in the grand scheme of things, they mean nothing in comparison to our health and happiness and are completely worthless to us personally at end of our lives. However, we may not see things the same way when it comes to the people we love and care for. This misunderstanding is twofold:

- Firstly, non-attachment to another person does not mean to wish them out of your life or care if they are in your life or not. The meaning in this context can easily be explained with the example of a possessive mother who never wants her children to spread their wings and leave home. A mother who gets jealous when the child makes other relationships is unhealthy and not based on true love. A mother who attaches herself (emotionally, cognitively and physically) to her children like a possession she owns outright is not expressing true love. Conversely, a mother with no attachment can take great joy in seeing her children grow into independent adults.

LOVE

Attachment says: I want you to make me happy.

Love says: I want you to be happy.

•   Secondly, the mistake is to also associate attachment with love, when in fact, to be unattached to someone you love is a critical element of love itself. For example, to force someone to remain in a relationship when they wish to leave is not love so we must be careful to distinguish between attachment and love. True love is to allow someone to be free to attain happiness wherever this may be and even at the expense of our own heartache perhaps.

3. DESIROUS ATTACHMENT TO FUTURE OBJECTS

Like desirous attachment to past objects, desirous attachment to future objects is to dedicate mental attention upon that which has yet to come into existence. We subconsciously spend much of our energy, mental dedication and emotions lusting non-existent objects. Remember, where our attention goes our energy flows, so perhaps you can glimpse the absurdity of attaching ourselves both psychologically and emotionally onto that which is not present. In fact, the very nature of this attachment will make our current position in life perceived as less desirable which in turn impacts our level of contentment and happiness. It is therefore, such desirous attachments to future object that continually make us discontented and always desiring more and to be somewhere other than where we are in the present moment.

Again, it is important to distinguish between desiring a future life of virtuous qualities and that of a life full of material unvirtuous objects. For example, having a future vision of a life in which you are completely contented, at peace and happy is directly opposed to a vision of attaining a bigger house, faster car or lavish lifestyle.

Once more, it is necessary to make this clear. Money, or any external object, is not inherently bad or indeed good but it is our attachment to such things which is the cause of the issue. We attach ourselves emotionally to money and assets because we bestow them with emotions but, of course, this is impossible. If money were to provide happiness for example, where in the coin or note is happiness located? Equally, if money were inherently evil, where within money does this evil reside? Any second world object cannot contain positive or negative emotions, but we attach ourselves to them as if they do.

As you read on you will get deeper clarity on this subject and realise that if you are able to let go of desirous attachment to past, present and future objects, you can manifest all your desires and all the objects you wish for, however, you will not be attached to such things because you will have found the true source of complete contentment and happiness. All the material pleasure which will surround you will be an addition but not essential to your new-found state of complete satisfaction.

"It is obvious that most people's attention and energy is directed to their outer material world. It begs the question: How much energy do you have left in your inner world of thoughts and feelings to create a new reality? "

Dr. Joe Dispenza in *Becoming Supernatural*

CHAPTER 6

UNDERSTANDING DISSONANCE

A simple yet clever psychological experiment was carried out to investigate a phenomenon termed cognitive dissonance.

Participants were separated into two groups with the only difference between the groups being the amount they got paid for taking part. Group A were paid $20 whilst group B was paid only $5. Both groups were introduced to a plainly decorated room where a glass box with a visible rod running through the middle was placed on a table. On the end of the rod was a handle which the participants were asked to continually turn for a thirty-minutes and then report back on their experience. As the participants could clearly see that the turning of the rod did nothing, the task was deliberately dull.

The interesting part came from the reports given by the two groups. Group A participants, who were paid $20, said the experiment was pointless, boring and a waste of their time, whilst group B, who were paid just $5, described it as fascinating, beautifully meditative or artistic. Whereas group A stated the truth about the futile task, group B found things to justify their participation.

The reason this difference was found is due to cognitive dissonance. Group A got paid enough money to justify their waste of time whereas group B had to resolve the mental conflict within them by finding reasons to defend their involvement. In the minds of group B, the amount they got paid did not justify the reason why they spent a portion of their life on a fruitless activity and thus, they had to resolve this internal conflict by mentally searching for justification.

Cognitive dissonance is experienced when an individual holds two cognitions which are psychologically inconsistent. This mental conflict causes psychological discomfort which motivates the individual to find ways to justify one thought over the other to resolve and ease the psychological tension.

Cognitive dissonance is one of the reasons why people stick to beliefs or habits even when they know they are wrong or even contradictory. Psychologists believe the reason why people find it hard to create a new belief system is because beliefs are tied with our identity and sense of self. To change our beliefs therefore, is to change ourselves.

The truth therefore is very hard for some people to hear and they will often actively seek out ways to rationalise irrational beliefs and behaviours to help resolve the cognitive dissonance within them.

Equally, people will also provide irrational responses to that which is rational due to cognitive dissonance.

With this in mind, if you truly understand that nothing is pleasant or unpleasant in itself but merely seen a certain way because of your own mind, you must also appreciate that all feelings are created by you rather than outside of you.

In the same way our projection of feelings upon objects can cause us to discriminate against certain people or things in favour of other things, we must also recognise our ability to use the same behaviour to discriminate against our own negative emotions in favour of positive ones.

This is not to say that we can simply ignore such feelings, in fact, this is not how we become masters of our emotions but when you view an object or person as unpleasant, you should recognise your ability to discriminate against such thoughts. You can remind yourself, with conscious reasoning and awareness, that nothing outside of yourself holds your feelings and it is your mind which imputes feelings outside of yourself.

Stress, anger, hate, lust and all manner of destructive non-virtuous states of mind are your responsibility. Refrain from letting anger manifest and recognise it as a delusion of your mind. It only exists within your mind. Stop hatred from arising and recognise that there is nothing which inherently contains hate outside of your mind. When you feel inappropriate lust towards someone, stop and recognise that the feelings you have are not intrinsic within that person but a mere creation of your mind.

In this way you can train your mind to discriminate against non-virtuous feelings and harmful emotions to form a mental continuum which discriminates towards virtuous feelings such as love and compassion.

On occasions, perhaps even as you read this, you may think *"yes, but..."*.

"Yes, but they were horrible to me, so I hate them"

"Yes, but they treated my wrongfully, so I am angry"

"Yes, but my job is demanding, so I am stressed"

This is cognitive dissonance and you are attempting to justify your thoughts, beliefs and behaviours. On the one hand, you feel hatred, anger or stress. On the other hand, you instinctively know that hate, anger and stress is opposed to the highest intention for yourself which is to be happy and that it is you who creates such negative states. These two conflicting cognitions must be resolved to ease your psychological dis-ease, so you justify your feelings by assigning the blame onto objects, conditions or people. Once you really and fully comprehend that the emotions you feel do not live within an object, situation or person but within your own mind, you can start to let go of such attachment.

A person may have treated you unkindly or abusively and this fact does not change or excuse their actions, however, with mindful attention, analytical thought and understanding you will recognise that you do not have to harbour negative feelings towards them. Without negative feelings you are open to more virtuous states such as love and compassion. Perhaps not towards the individual who has wronged you, but it would allow you to be healthier and happier.

I recall working with a client who assigned her anger onto an individual who treated her very unkindly. The anger towards this person affected her health, her family, her relationships, her ability to cope and, of course, her happiness. Her mind held strong attachment to hate and her thoughts, speech and behaviours were infected. With understanding and effort, she recognised that, although the individual's actions were wrong and harmful, that person did not possess the hatred she felt, and she was, in fact, harming herself. With time and effort, she was able to let her attachment go.

She called me one day to excitedly report that she had just walked past the person in question completely free from hate and negative feelings. She said she felt in control, empowered and free.

Whilst you have hate in your mind you cannot experience love. With anger in your mind you cannot experience peace. Whilst you manifest any negative emotions within your mind you cannot have happiness.

CHAPTER 7

UNDERSTANDING ASPIRATIONS

For some people, aspirations, wishes and desires are good qualities to possess whilst for others it is a bad trait to have. The truth is both views are correct. Some of the things aspire and desire will enhance our personal development, happiness and life satisfaction whilst others will impede our personal and spiritual progress.

Every one of us wants to have certain things within our lives and behind all aspirations is the motivation to increase happiness. Whether you wish to have children, have more money, drive a nicer car, find the right relationship or whatever you aspire to gain, the underlying aspiration is to improve your level of happiness.

We can say that the desire to attain more financial stability is not about the attainment of happiness but a wish to offer a sense of security and ability to provide for the needs of loved ones. But if we are successful in attaining financial security and free from worry about provision of loved ones, we would feel happy. We can say that our wish to have children and start a family is to give life more meaning and purpose. A life with more meaning and purpose would be a happier life than one without it. We can even say that our aspiration to lose fat is motivated by our wish to be healthier, have more energy and live longer. With increased health, vitality and longevity we also create more happiness. Regardless of what we aspire to attain, the ultimate motivation and highest intention is to increase happiness.

As already discussed, if you fully understand that emotions cannot be found in objects or anything outside of your mind, you can recognise the error in pursuing happiness outside of yourself also. Happiness is thought to be found by the attainment of objects and, just as with negative emotions, we assign pleasant feelings onto objects and therefore want them more. Of course, as we all can testify, when we achieve this desire, we either yearn for more objects or, eventually, we resign to the belief that life consists only of brief moments of happiness and, no matter what external things we gain, lasting contentment, peace and enduring satisfaction cannot be found.

If we understand that objects are not endowed with feelings and therefore, no object is inherently pleasant or unpleasant why attach our happiness to them?

Furthermore, when we are unhappy we notice it and naturally aspire to move away from the perceived source of sadness. As we impute objects or circumstances with the feeling of happiness, as if they are the source of happiness, we pursue more objects and situations which are believed to improve our mood.

The true aspiration and ultimate goal in life is happiness and to find this we must search within, not outside.

UNDERSTANDING DELUDED ASPIRATIONS

'Deluded': To believe something which is not true

One of the common aspirations in life is to have more money even though, the more you have of it the more stress, worry, distrust and anxiety you are likely to have. For example, lottery winners are commonly found to end up less happy when compared to levels of happiness before their winning ticket and yet, we still dream of seeing our numbers come up on a Saturday night. We are told subconsciously, through adverts, media and marketing that our lives can be significantly improved via the gathering of more material possessions, better gadgets and bigger objects and we believe such messages. On the other side, we are also told our entire country owes billions if not trillions and we have to cut back and pay more tax to keep us afloat.

Even though evidence clearly shows financial wealth does little to improve our happiness, we still believe it to be the Holy Grail. The subtle and overt installation of this belief via marketing and media has caused many of us to focus outside of ourselves for happiness. This has led to most Western countries becoming wealthier and mental health issues, such as depression, to increase at the same time.

The American Society of Aesthetic Plastic Surgery reported a forty-four percent increase in cosmetic surgery between 2003 and 2004. In England the trend is similar with £50 million more being spent on cosmetic surgery than tea. However, research suggests, just like the attainment of all other external assets, the satisfaction initially gained fades quickly. The issue is rarely external, it is internal.

In times of financial austerity, we are told our country is in debt by the tune of billions or trillions which, of course, sounds very frightening. But who are we indebted to exactly? If the government controls the money, then surely, they can simply wipe the debt. Whilst the Governments responsibility is to attempt to balance the books, every British pound and every US Dollar is not theirs and, by definition, not ours either.

Money in the UK is printed by the Bank of England whilst in the USA it is the Federal Reserve Bank. Both are private organisations. The governments do not own these banks and therefore must request money in the same way we acquire loans from our personal bank.

The money you have in your purse, pocket or wallet is part of a loan to your Government. For each Pound or Dollar there is interest attached. Therefore, money is debt. With this system, our country can never pay off the debt owed because there is not enough money to do so. The monetary system is a system of debt. The more money there is the more debt there is.

"If there were no debt in our money system there wouldn't be any money"

Marriner Eccles, Governor of the Federal Reserve Bank (1941)

This is how our monetary system works. The government borrows money from the central bank and the bank asks for interest on each note printed knowing that it can never be repaid because the only money in circulation is that which they lent in the first place.

The most inspired part of this system is the fact that rarely does physical money actually changes hands. The only money in existence is that which has been printed. So, to make money without printing more of it, it is simply created from nothing which we see in bank statements and at the cash point.

When you get paid, receive a bank loan or mortgage, we have a mental image of money physically being gathered from one place and transported into your account. However, it is a computerized system of numbers not bank notes. They literally type in the digits and the money appears in your bank. Of course, no actual physical money is transferred because there is a finite amount available so to make more money, it is created on a computer screen. However, your loan has interest attached to it of course which you pay back to the bank and the bank deducts the equivalent numbers from your loan. No more actual money has been created just the changing of digits on a computer.

In 1969, Jerome Daily successfully fought a court case against a Minnesota bank because they wanted to repossess his home due to arrears in mortgage payments. Jerome defended and won his case because the bank lent him money which they did not physically have to lend. As he successfully contested in court, the bank merely created the funds by adding electronic digits to his account. Indeed, this is the exact same system as cryptocurrency such as the Bitcoin except for the fact that this is a self-regulating system which no one owns.

It is estimated that if everyone wished to physically hold the money they have in their bank account there would be a shortfall equating to ten times the amount of physical money available on the entire planet.

I include this section to help direct our focus onto the true source of happiness and expose our delusions and illusions. Not only is money an illusory system of debt rather than wealth so too is the attachment of happiness to it an illusion of mind.

I stress once more, there is nothing wrong with wealth per se, and the monetary system is what we use to provide comforts and meet our basic needs such as shelter, warmth, clothing and food but it is the belief that having more equals more happiness which is the issue.

It is interesting to note that there seems to be a universal 'cut off point' when it comes to happiness and wealth. Studies of wealth show that, above earnings of £50,000 per annum, happiness levels decrease significantly. This suggests that once our basic needs are met and we have little financial concerns in this area, additional income makes us less contented.

You can aspire to live in a beach condo and drive an expensive car, there is nothing wrong with any such aspirations, unless you believe these things will provide you with increased and lasting happiness. The root cause of a rich man's happiness will be despite his wealth not because of it. Rather than aspiring to make money to gain more belongings, use it to gain more life experiences, such as travelling and personal growth, because this is scientifically understood to be the best use of money if you want more happiness.

CHAPTER 8

UNDERSTANDING CONTROL

I used to live along a sleepy country road in Stroud, Gloucestershire. It was February, the temperature had plummeted overnight and there were a few inches of snow on the ground. Not considering the conditions on the road I habitually drove my usual route to work, down a country lane, through a small township and up the other side to meet the main road into Cheltenham.

The narrow country roads were not accessible to gritting trucks and I began to realise the error of my decision as I slid down to the township avoiding the brakes as much as possible and slowing through my gears. Without four-wheel drive, the wheels slipped at the slightest touch of the accelerator and skated with every touch of the brake. Approaching the short but steep accent up to the main road I knew I had to make it in the same gear because if I dropped down a gear the wheels would simply spin. So, I purposefully picked up speed and upped to the top gear to gain more traction, but it was not fast enough and half way up I was going too slow. I had no choice but to change down a gear and hope for the best. As quickly as I could to maintain momentum, one foot came off the accelerator whilst the other slammed down on the clutch before applying the accelerator once again. The car lurched forward as the engine cried out. I gained a meter or two before the rear wheels began to spin. I depressed the accelerator pedal to the floor as the engine and tyres began to scream. Smoke and the smell of burning rubber began to pass my window and fill my nostrils, but I remained stationary, wheels whirling on the spot.

After a few more wishful seconds, I accepted my fate. Releasing the throttle, I began to roll backwards down the hill. Furiously pumping the breaks only helped prevent total freefall. My car was now effectively a sledge sashaying rapidly downhill. Twisted in my seat glaring out of the rear window with one hand darting right and left on the steering wheel, I tried desperately to navigate the car but it continued to gather pace and there was no way I could stop it. The choice was either to crash now or crash later at an even greater speed.

With my heart tearing through my chest, with wide eyes I watched the Cotswold stone wall skyrocket towards the rear of my car. I turned back around and braced for impact.

If you have experienced anything similar, you will also know the feeling of being completely out of control. Feeling utterly helpless in the knowledge that there is nothing you can do but accept your fate. This is an extremely frightening and intensely stressful experience.

Having a sense of control is one of the psychological essentials in life. Feeling in control of yourself, your health, your home environment, your children, your career, your relationships, your emotions or your future, is known to be a key element for life satisfaction.

"I have taught one thing and one thing only, dukkha and the cessation of dukkha."

Buddha Shakyamuni

Dukkha is a Sanskrit term commonly translated as emotional dis-ease, anxiety and dissatisfaction. Dukkha is therefore a very familiar state we can recognise in our fast paced and schedule driven world.

To reduce dukkha is our main mission in life because without stress, worry and suffering we would be relaxed, in control and happy. Regardless of whether we are consciously aware of it or not, all our actions, behaviours, wants and desires are aimed at reducing dukkha. The highest intention in life is therefore driven to reduce emotional dis-ease and by association increase our level of happiness.

Once again, for most of us we are highly focused on moving away from the things which make us unhappy rather than concentrating on the dedication to move towards the true inner cause of happiness. It is no surprise therefore, that our familiarity with life is mostly stress, worry, troubles, struggles, emotional suffering and minimal sense of control, because that is what our mind is absorbed by most of the time. With a mind dedicated to moving 'away from' our present life we enter into a repetitive rollercoaster of dis-ease followed by reprieve, before returning to dis-ease once again.

To further compound this problem, all features of life are transient, on the move and always altering. To find relief from life's worries, troubles, stressors and fears, we persistently attempt to control that which is uncontrollable because they, including ourselves, are in a constant state of change. In this sense all matter, and material things, are impermanent due to the ceaseless state of transformation, and yet, we try to stabilize it, hold it still and gain control of it. The shoes you adore today for example, will provide less pleasure in the near future as they gradually disintegrate along with your attraction for them.

Instinctively we recognise that once in control of ourselves and our lives, freedom from dukkha will be found. However, our efforts are directed to move away from sufferings rather than towards bliss. Our minds are attached to an external world which is in a constant state of change and therefore uncontrollable.

Moment by moment our body changes, the weather changes, nature changes, people change. Circumstances in one instant are not the same as the next and today will not the same as tomorrow. The money we have today will be different this evening. All external realities are impermanent. How can we expect to tame such a fickle nature of life?

Many of us live our entire lives desperately attempting to hold tightly onto that which naturally alters over time and this causes dis-ease. We attach ourselves to past objects, present objects and objects we do not possess. We attempt to control our ageing body but of course, this is a futile task which cannot be won. We attempt to manipulate our circumstances, but each day is different and forever changing. We attempt to control the environment and surround ourselves with furnishings and material possessions, and yet, our tastes will change over time, fashion changes and the objects themselves change. We attempt to control relationships, but people are independent, with minds and emotions which we cannot control. The economy will always fluctuate, investments will be gained and lost, and financial situations can quickly change.

Each time we fail to grasp strongly onto the impermanent it changes, and we lose grip once again. This constant venture to control the uncontrollable is like trying to catch a fly. With its speed of unpredictable movement, we flail and dart around struggling to catch it. When we think we may have seized it, it will fly away the moment we open our hand to look.

Once we realise that we cannot control the external world via our external actions we start to look inwardly to find peace, harmony and control.

Cessation from dukkha cannot be found from attempts to control the external world because it is impermanent and thus, uncontrollable, but if we move towards self-mastery of body and mind a new and profound level of control can be revealed.

CHAPTER 9

UNDERSTANDING INTENTION

Aspirations are dedicated to achieving a desired goal but does not necessitate action or effort. Intention on the other hand involves taking physical action, verbal action or mental action. However, as we now have a deeper understanding of the mind, we can recognise that all actions begin with the mind.

Intention is the mental function by which we take physical, verbal or mental action. Actions carry us to a desired destination, but it is our intention which drives us. Equally, our actions can be good or bad, kind or unkind, healthy or unhealthy, virtuous or unvirtuous, we can therefore conclude that it is from our intentions where health, happiness and wellbeing can derive.

Intention is the starting point for your development. You can intend to continue to pay attention to what you do not wish in your life or you can intend to make conscious effort to redirect your attention towards what you do wish to manifest. You can also intend to focus on the external world or intend to pay attention to the internal world. Until you have the intent to direct your attention towards the mastery of your mind, how can you begin to change?

For the resultant actions of your intentions to be successful, you need to have belief. With understanding you can develop stronger beliefs and it was my intention for you to have gained sufficient understanding by this point in the book to believe, at least in the possibility, that you can make transformational and lasting positive changes.

Without belief your intentions will be weak at best and therefore your actions will be fleeting or half-hearted. Weak intentions followed up with corresponding actions limit your potential. In short, you must fully believe that you have the potential to become the master of your life and creator of your ideal future.

With strong beliefs comes resilient intentions. With resilient intentions come influential physical and metaphysical actions. The result of such a combination is strong attraction and rapid manifestation.

CHAPTER 10

UNDERSTANDING BELIEFS

Our beliefs are formed by past experiences, influential people and other sources of information such as the media. Certainly nowadays, technology allows us access to masses of information literally within our hand and therefore our beliefs are increasingly influenced by news feeds and social media.

In the early eighties Eric Johnson and Amos Tversky conducted an experiment involving two groups of university students. One group was provided with negative news stories whilst the others were issued with positive news stories. After a short period of time, the students were asked what they believed about their own chances of being the victim of a crime or tragedy. Unsurprisingly perhaps, the students who were reading negative news believed that they were highly likely to be personally affected by crime or disaster whereas those exposed to happier news feeds were far less concerned.

At the time of writing this, since the attacks on the Twin Towers in 2001, there have been under one-hundred deaths directly linked to extremist activity in the USA and less so in the UK. Putting these statistics into perspective, each year in the USA, roughly double this amount of deaths are caused by peanut allergies. Indeed, it is also true that a whopping seventy-eight thousand people die annually due to smoking related diseases.

Of course, I am certainly not demeaning any death as I see all life as precious and sacred. I am using this example to highlight the power of the beliefs we form, and the influence media has on our world perception. For instance, a friend of mine became so frightened about the prolific messages of "terror" they stopped going on holiday due to anxiety of flying. They became paranoid and suspicious of anyone who "looked Muslim". This friends' life became one of distrust, stress and fear when the real threat to his life were the cigarettes in his pocket, and yet, this habit was not seen as threatening to the same degree.

Fundamentalist Muslims involved in attacks against the West account for 0.0003% of the Muslim population and yet, because of the way attacks are reported and the coverage dedicated to underline the fear and racially laced narrative, the Media creates a national and international view of the world which is far removed from reality.

On the flipside, it is also known that people with a happier, optimistic world view, tend to achieve more because they are not restricted by negative beliefs or fears. These individuals are found to be more persistent when faced with difficult tasks, they have a more engaging social life, take opportunities to travel and try new experiences for example.

The beliefs we have about ourselves and the world directly influence what we achieve and gain from life. In this sense, beliefs manifest into a self-fulfilling prophesy whereby we behave according to our belief systems. If beliefs are limiting or negative we can learn to become helpless.

A brutal and, in my opinion, unethical example of learned helplessness was demonstrated in a study which put rats in a bucket of water. Without help, rats were found to give up swimming and drown well before physical exhaustion. However, if a rat is picked out of the water and then placed back in, they will keep swimming until they can swim no more.

Of course, it stands to reason that if you believe there is nothing to be gained from attempting to achieve something then you are not going to attempt to attain it or may give up at the slightest effort or hurdle.

When a person is instructed to be deliberately negative within a group task, it will significantly decrease the groups chances of success. Equally, if a single person remains positive, it is shown to create positive beliefs within the group and they are much more likely to succeed. In fact, the consistent findings from such studies indicate that beliefs are the greatest predictor of success, more so than intelligence, academic achievements or experience.

One thing we consistently seem to overlook regarding our beliefs is personal choice and control. You have a choice to believe your beliefs. The beliefs you hold about yourself and your life are not set, you can challenge and change them.

In evolutionary terms, habits are formed by a part of the brain called the Basal Ganglia. This prehistoric area of the brain encodes behaviours into automated responses to external triggers. For instance, "When I feel 'X' I behave 'Y'". This automation allows the rest of the brain to process other more conscious tasks such as paying attention to a conversation whilst subconsciously driving the car.

With this understanding we can change begin our negative habits. When you feel a certain unhelpful way, take a moment and think about what is causing you to feel that way, what thoughts do you have, and do you believe the thoughts. Ask if the beliefs are true, justified and accurate. What evidence do you have to support your belief and what alternative beliefs could also be true?

Understanding that it is your beliefs which can keep you stuck in an unfavourable situation, habitual behaviour cycle or prevent you from getting the most of yourself and your life, is key. Understanding that you do, in fact, have a choice should be motivation enough for you to start making positive changes. Do you believe that negative thoughts and feelings are echoes from your past and will continue to be reinforced in a self-fulfilling prophesy? Do you believe that there is more to the external world than meets the eye and that your thoughts, feelings and actions will manifest your future both cognitively and physically?

What we believe becomes our thoughts, feelings, behaviours and our perception of realty. Not only do we listen to what we are told and tell ourselves but the cells within our body are also listening.

CHAPTER 11

MIND OVER MATTER

We know that our own thoughts and beliefs can influence our external, subjective second world reality because we know about the placebo effect. Countless experiments have shown how powerful the mind can be at influencing our experiences and feelings.

The placebo effect was first reported when a drug company tested a new pain relief tablet which stimulated the release of natural opioids such as endorphins and dopamine. To compare the effectiveness of the new drug, experimenters told a separate group of people that they too were taking pain relief medication, when in fact, they were given an inert chalk tablet. The results baffled the experimenters as the group who took the dummy tablet reported just as much pain relief as the group who took the real drug.

Many scientists dismissed the suggestion that beliefs could produce actual reduction in pain and, considering the reduction of pain was subjective reports from individual experience, objective reduction could not be verified. In other words, just because someone says they feel less pain does not mean they did.

Undeterred, the experimenters refined the test, this time extracting blood samples to objectively measure levels of opioids within the blood of participant groups before and after they were given their tablets. As expected the blood results showed significant increases in opioid serum levels in the group which took the real pain relief drug, however, the same increase in opioids were also seen in the control group too. The results further suggesting that the physiological process of opioid release could be induced by the belief that pain medication has been ingested. Pain could not only be controlled by the mind but, moreover, the pain relief experienced was not simply psychosomatic but a real physiological response.

Furthermore, when the experiment was carried out without informing the subjects what the drug was for, the 'real drug' group experienced pain relief whilst the control group did not. Further proving that the effect recorded was belief driven and not connected to the chalk tablet.

Everyone had to concede that belief can reduce pain and cause cells within the brain to release the relevant neurotransmitters to desensitize the pain receptor cells throughout the body, even when the pill contains absolutely no active ingredient.

In another experiment, pregnant women experiencing severe morning sickness were told they had been given a new anti-nausea drug when in fact it was an in-active placebo pill. A small device was also used to measure stomach activity known to be associated with feelings of nausea and sickness. A statistically significant number of the women not only reported relief from sickness, the measurements showed a corresponding physiological response too.

In 2002, sixty patients on the list for knee surgery were finally called up for their long-awaited procedure. In the hospital they were taken through all the usual medical procedures from consultations with the surgeon prior to entering theatre, standard forms to sign and skimpy gowns to adorn. What was believed to be post-surgery, patients were shown footage of the procedure by the consultant to show how well the surgery went. Ostensibly showing a duty of care, these patients were contacted nearly a year after discharge from hospital to see how their symptoms were. All patients reported significant improvement in symptoms and many had returned to similar levels of activity achieved before their knee issues. However, no surgery took place.

What these, and many countless studies show, is that the placebo effect is not just psychological, but beliefs cause physiological changes within the body. In fact, around forty percent of patient improvement is thought to be down to placebo.

The mind is a powerful tool which we can use to heal or harm ourselves. Where our attention goes, energy flows and if we are consistently telling our body negative messages then we not only reinforce the cognitive filter of belief which supports this message we can also manifest symptoms and real physiological changes to match.

We know this from our own experiences. If we feel stressed and become acutely aware that this is likely to be increasing our heart rate and blood pressure, our attention is directed to this area of the body along with our energy. This in turn triggers the release of hormones such as adrenaline and cortisol which physiologically increase our heart rate and blood pressure. Our own mental actions, intentions and directed thoughts, have stimulated and manifested a physiological response within our body.

What we search for we find. If you search for discomfort within your body you will find it and if you continue to focus on it, it will get worse. If you search for stress, you will find stressors. If you search for pain your will find it. In a basic sense this is the essence of attraction and a self-fulfilling prophecy, which we will discuss in detail shortly.

The capacity of the mind creates an internal environmental reality and we respond accordingly. The cognitive filters we have formed creates an environment equal to the perception. If we believe the world to be a cruel and harsh place then we delete, distort and generalise information to fit in with that world view. Conversely, if we believe it to be a playground of opportunity and wonder then we delete, distort and generalise the information to create and reinforce that perception. The same occurs within our own body on a physical level.

EPIGENETICS

Prior to current scientific understanding, psychologist held the view that the mind and body are separate entities. Psychological theories clearly highlighted the indirect effect of mind upon the body and body upon the mind, but neither were believed to be synonymous. For example, if a factory machine has a faulty part it effects the entire machine, but the part is separate from the rest of the machine. The medical model was, and still is to a larger degree, based on the same mechanical and fragmented view of the body and mind. If you have a swelling you are given anti-inflammatory drugs to mechanically reduce inflammation. If you have depression you may take antidepressants. If you have acid reflux you ingest a liquid to neutralize stomach acid. If you are experiencing pain, you take pain relief medication to block the pain receptor cites. If you have a knee problem, you have surgery to remove the issue.

Although these treatments are seen to neutralize the cause, in fact, they are masking the cause by reducing the systems. The body, mind, behaviours and environment are largely dismissed within the medical model. For instance, the swelling in your foot, for which you take medication, could be caused by the shoes you are wearing. The depression you are suffering from may be caused by thoughts and feelings of loss in your life. The heartburn you are experiencing could be caused by the food you are consuming. The pain in your knee could be caused by weak thigh muscles. To look at the body in a more holistic manner rather than separate mechanical parts we can see that thoughts, beliefs, behaviours and environment all have an influence on our health and wellbeing.

Traditional biology viewed the human body the same way. If a part of the body is defective, the part at 'blame' could be modified or replaced to resolve the issue rather than viewing the body as unified with mind, body, behaviours and environment.

Traditional biology viewed the body and its cells as separated parts which work independently to produce a complete working system. For example, the heart plays its role to keep the body functional by pumping blood around the body, but it is a distinct component of the body. Similarly, the liver is also part of the body-machine, its primary function is to filter the blood pumped by the heart whilst the muscles cells extracted the oxygen and nutrients within the blood. The brain is the cognizer and narrator of information via the central nervous system. Each body part functions together to make the body work, like cogs in a watch, but none were traditionally believed to be fundamentally connected or holistic in nature.

The Darwinian approach to our evolution and hereditary expressions of genes has long been held as the predictor of behaviour, personality, disease and, in fact, all aspects of human beings. It was believed that we are a controlled by-product of our genes and we are at mercy of our genetic makeup. The Darwinian view states that we have no control over our destiny. The fate of our physical and psychological health, our life expectancy, our personality and even how we would likely die, was destined within our genetic code.

Although quiet rumblings could be heard at nature verse nurture debates, the influence of environment was dwarfed by those who believed all answers could be found by decoding the human genome.

In 1990 the Human Genome Project was launched with a primary goal to sequence the three thousand million base pairs of genes which make up human blueprint. The implications of this project were immense but also worrisome. Drugs could be developed to deactivate genes known to cause illness and disease. Food crops could be genetically manipulated to produce hardier plants or ability to increase nutritional value. Discovering what genes produced blue eyes, curly hair, athleticism, certain personality traits or intelligence set the scene for potential 'designer' babies.

After thirteen years of collaborative work from scientists all over the world, in 2003 the number of gene sequences found were several thousand short.

In other words, the amount of genetic code was found to be considerably too small to account for the complexity of a human being. For instance, an individual could have his or her entire genome mapped but it would not look like an identifiable replica of themselves, in fact, it could be anyone.

Studies show that an individual can hold the gene for depression, for example, and yet, not show any symptoms. Equally, people have been found to have all the genetic coding of a psychopath, and yet, very few showed physical or psychological expression of this genetic trait.

This was a major blow to the Darwinian hypothesis and geneticists. It would seem that our body must be influenced by something other than just our genes and so attention changed towards the pioneering work of epigenesists.

Epigenetics is the study of genetics and the influence environment has on genes. Contrary to the standard biological paradigm, epigenetic research shows that we are not in fact completely governed by our genes.

Like the nervous system is the Control Centre of our body, then, according to research findings in the field of epigenetics, our cells are the managers and our own personal thoughts and beliefs is the CEO.

"It is not gene directed hormones or neurotransmitters that control our bodies and our minds; our beliefs control our bodies, our minds and thus our lives...Positive thoughts have a profound effect on behaviour and genes, but only when they are in harmony with the subconscious programming. And negative thoughts have an equally powerful effect. When we recognise how these positive and negative beliefs control our biology, we can use this knowledge to create lives filled with health and happiness"

Dr Bruce Lipton in Biology of Belief

Stem cells are cells before they have assigned themselves to a specific role and therefore could reproduce to become any part of the body. Stem cells are therefore termed multipotent stem cells. Dr

Lipton, arguably one of the trailblazers for epigenetic research, placed a stem cell in a certain culture to find that they reproduced to form liver cells. He then took another stem cell and placed it in a slightly different culture and the cell reproduced into skin cells. Each time Dr Lipton altered the environment in which the stem cell was placed, the cell responded to form a different biological function. This experiment shows that the external environment in which our cells grow determines how they behave.

It is similarly interesting to know that if a mother of an unborn child perceives the world to be life threatening and fearful, her child is statistically likely to be born with fifty-two percent decrease in IQ compared to his or her mother. Effectively, the mothers message to her fetus is that the world outside is one to be fearful of and thus, survival characteristics are priority. The unborn child develops more aggression, an increased sense of self-preservation, physical muscularity, endurance, agility, selfishness and other survival-based traits over intelligence. In other words, the mother's thoughts, beliefs and perceived or real experiences directly informed the cells of her developing fetus.

Our genetic coding, or DNA, is found within the chromosomes within our cells. However, a chromosome does not just contain DNA, it also has proteins which encase the DNA like a coat.

Think of it like a bank. The cell is the bank, and inside which is a vault (chromosomes). Each piece of gold (our DNA) is kept further secured within a protein draw cabinet within the vault.

When a draw within a vault is opened, the qualities of the gold, whether it is a gold bullion, gold necklace or a goblet, can be seen. When a draw is closed, there is no way to determine what is in it.

Like the gold within a vault, if a gene within a DNA strand is covered by protein, the draw is shut, and the gene is switched off because it cannot be seen to determine the qualities. If, on the other hand, there is no protein, then the draw is open, the gene can be seen and therefore, it is switched on and expressed.

Now, here is the really interesting part...

The genetic draws within our cells can be opened (switched on) or closed (switched off) by the environmental signals we send it through our thoughts and beliefs. If we think optimistically our internal environment will reflect this with biochemicals that produce positive feelings of joy, love and happiness. In such a situation the message being sent to our cells is that the environment outside the body is safe, healthy and secure. In turn, the happiness gene is uncovered by the chromosome's protein coat and the gene is switched on, giving us a natural, genetic bias towards increased enjoyment and satisfaction.

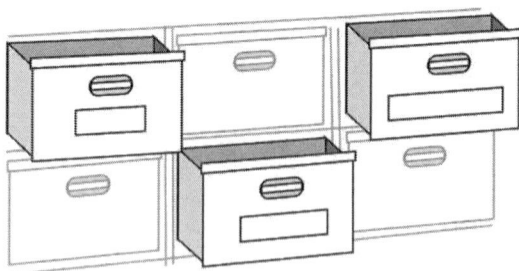

Of course, the opposite is also true. If we are frequently feeling stressed, worried or angry, the respective hormones are released into our internal environment and our cell receptor sites are being told that the environment outside is harsh, dangerous and full of threats. Consequently, the relevant genes are revealed to enhance our bias towards anxiousness and aggression, which of course means reduced positive emotions, physical functioning and psychological wellbeing.

We personally control our health and wellbeing via our thoughts and beliefs. What we most frequently tell the cells about the world outside affects the environment inside. An inner environment flushed with cortisol, adrenaline, feelings of aggression and so forth, paints a picture of the outside world to our genes and they respond accordingly. The environment we create will either makes us fit, healthy and happy or weak, sick and miserable at the genetic level.

For example, when the gene for breast cancer was discovered there was of course huge concern for thousands of females who were highly likely to have passed on this gene. However, further research showed that only five percent of cancer cases could be directly linked to a gene. It was therefore proposed that the remaining ninety-five percent of cases were likely to be environmentally triggered via our thoughts, beliefs and chemical exposure from diet and so forth.

In fact, further epigenetic research now suggests that this process not only happens to DNA but on all cells throughout the body. In other words, all our cells react and behave in accordance to the signals we send it. Healthy thoughts, healthy beliefs, healthy behaviours equal healthy cells. Unhealthy thoughts, unhealthy beliefs and unhealthy behaviours equals unhealthy cells.

It is no longer just about what we put in our body or physically expose it to, it is equally about what we think and believe. What we tell our cells via the thoughts we have about our life, the beliefs we have about ourselves and what we put in our body, paints a picture of the outside world and our cells respond in kind.

We are holistic beings rather than consisting of separated mechanical parts. The body and mind are not simply indirectly connected via their separate functions, the mind and body are one and the same. The body is the mind and the mind is the body. There are no separate parts. All is intricately connected as a whole.

Signals are being sent by our thoughts, beliefs and behaviours across our entire body and through every cell. Sequentially, our cells then send signals back to confirm, and conform, with the environmental signals they receive.

In 2008, Dr Robert Gamling surveyed nearly three thousand adults to ask what they believed about their future health status. Following these individuals, a number of years later it was found that those who believed they were at risk of heart disease were three times more likely to have had a heart attack compared to others, even after all other risk variables were considered.

It is also known from scientific studies that patients who are informed of their terminal illness will die statistically faster than those who are unaware of their condition. Conversely, Neal Krause from the University of Michigan found that people who frequently took time to wish another person to be healthy were found to improve their own health status when compared to those who wished others to become successful or wealthy for example.

It is well documented that fighter pilots are told throughout their training that they are the best of the best. This belief is purposefully drilled into them as a strategy to enable them to cope with high-speed and highly stressful combat situations. Perhaps this is why fighter pilots show significantly less nervous breakdowns when compared to any other section within the armed forces?

The old Darwinian approach suggested that those of us with superior genes are at an advantage. The survival of the fittest competition is now known to give advantage to those with the most harmonious, life enhancing and controlled minds rather than athleticism and physical strength.

"Perhaps the only limits to the human mind are those we believe in"

Willis Harman. President of the Institute of Noetic Sciences (1977 – 1997)

If our thoughts can influence physical objects within our own body can they do the same for physical objects outside of us?

WHAT WE FOCUS ON GROWS

"What we focus on grows" is not just a figurative statement but a literal one too. Studies investigating the effects of meditation showed neural growth in areas of the brain associated with directed thoughts. If a meditator focused their intention toward the happiness of human beings, they are found to have enlarged portions of the brain associated with wanting to help. Similar results are seen in those using meditation to focus their mind on an object exclusively which is reflected by the growth of an area of the brain responsible for paying attention.

One study showed thirteen-percent increase in right arm bicep muscle size and strength just by imagining flexing the arm over a few weeks. Another study showed increases in breast size via hypnosis and many studies of athletes show mental visualization of a physical action creates marked improvements in muscle agility and speed. From such studies and numerous like them, it is now accepted that your mind has the capability to manifest physical changes within your body, in fact, you have been doing this for most of your life via your thoughts. Also, it is fully understood that you can rewire your brain to think, feel and behave however you choose.

Before the millennium, the structure of the brain was widely believed to be fixed at some point during our teenage years. However, in 2000, cognitive neuroscientist Eleanor Maguire and her team scanned the brains of London workers to discover something odd. Compared to other people, the brain structure of London cabbies were consistently different.

The MRI scans showed a significant difference in an area of the brain called the hippocampus. Moreover, this anomaly was found in a very specific area of the hippocampus and the size of this part of the brain correlated with the length of time the taxi driver had been in the job. In other words, this part of the brain continued to develop as time went on.

The hippocampus plays a key role in spatial memory and navigation. Much like Taxi drivers, animals who find their way around a large territory show similar brain structures.

The highly significant outcome of this study was the proof that we can rewire and even grow specific areas of the brain via experiences, learning, behaviours and thought.

To become a licensed cab driver in London you must first pass an exam known as The Knowledge. This examination tests the knowledge of London roads and ability to successfully navigate best routes. Studying for this notoriously hard exam changes and rewires the neural structure of the students' brain and as a result they will think differently and see things differently.

Numerous studies have since confirmed our own ability to rewire 'grey matter' and create new or stronger neural pathways just by the way we focus our mental attention and thoughts.

The fact we can change our neurology, rewire our own brain and therefore change our cognitive filter systems means we can change our view of the world.

No longer can we blame our personality for unhelpful habits and traits. If you want to think differently, then, with initially effort and dedication, you can physically change your brain and the world will be viewed accordingly.

As one of the world's leading experts in neurobiology and treatment of anxiety disorders, Dennis Charney says:

"Through psychological exercises, we can enhance the functioning of our brain and help it to enable its fullest capacity"

CHAPTER 12

FIRST WORLD REALITY

It is necessary to take a relevant but slight side step at this juncture and talk about the concept of time.

There is an Amazonian tribe called Amondawa which lacks any linguistic reference for time. In a BBC report, Chris Sinha, a professor of psychology of language at the University of Portsmouth said:

"What we don't find in this tribe is a notion of time as being independent of the events which are occurring; they don't have a notion of time which is something the events occur in"

Words such as "yesterday", "Year" or "Next week" have no meaning to this tribe which means they have no concept of events having past or events coming up in the future. We could assign this lack of time to the tribe being primitive but perhaps they have a more accurate view of reality than we do? Time is a man-made, or should I say, mind-made concept.

Desirous attachment to past, present and future objects keeps us mentally, physically and emotionally devoted to spending energy and mental focus in realities which do not exist. If you have read any self-help books or listened to any of my audiobooks, you will no doubt have heard about the concept of being present in the moment and being in the here and now.

It is no coincidence that this concept appears so frequently because it is vital, in fact, critical for personal spiritual growth and development. Entering the void of the present moment, where time and objects do not exist to the mind, is the door through which transcendence, spiritual connection and manifestation of virtuous desires will arise.

But let's not get ahead of ourselves. For now, let us once again provide knowledge and understanding to help fire and wire neurons and help you disconnect from old neural pathways to form new connections which are more aligned with the Ultimate Truth of reality.

We now understand the thought, feeling and behaviour cycle is predicted by our neural structuring and cognitive filters which, in turn, are reflections of our past. Therefore, our past creates thoughts which forecast our future and yet, neither past or future truly exist. The past is a time already experienced and no longer exists. The future has not happened yet and therefore is non-existent.

This fact brings new light onto the illusions of our second world reality as we realise that we live in a mind created world which does not truly exist. Thoughts cannot materialise in the present moment because the here and now is neither past or future.

Think about this: every thought you have, by its very nature, must and can only be manufactured from a past event which has been and gone or a future event which is yet to occur. Even within a second, such as watching a tree swing in the breeze perhaps, the event must occur first before we can think about it.

Time is a man-made and mind-made concept and an echo of our illusory second world view rather than the true first world reality.

The time on a clock face is a man-made system to provide organization to our day based on the earths solar cycle. The sensation of time passing is partly due to this ingrained concept of a twenty-four-hour day and our thoughts which continually live in moments gone and moments yet to materialise.

This is another illusion to add to an already illusory perception. However, there is another world which exists, an alternative reality which can be found in between past and future, in the present moment. This is the place here and now, where new beginnings reside, where the unknown becomes known, where we attain the ultimate goal of lasting happiness, where we can transform our mind and manifest our desires.

In 1905, Einstein's Special Theory of Relativity showed that time is relative and dependent upon the motion of the observer. The person walking along a moving train carriage for example, will seem to be moving much faster to the individual observing from the station platform as the train passes by. Similarly, if we were to leave earth in a rocket at close to the speed of light, for every year that passed for us, many years would have passed on earth. Time is therefore reliant on other objects. If we were floating through the darkness of deep space, we would have no concept of time or movement because there would be no object to compare ourselves to. Now we can recognise that this concept of time is subjective and dependent upon objects around us, so without objects, there would be no time and without time there would be no objects (Stay with me as we will discuss this more in the next section).

We hold a mental concept that time is moving along in a linear direction. One second is followed by another second, one hour followed by another hour and so forth. However, this is a man-made concept created by the division of the earth's rotation around the sun into units we call time. One solar cycle we call a day or twenty-four hours. However, this is just a measurement tool which gives us the perception of time passing by. The truth is, it is just a man-made measurement to enable us to organise our day.

We also have an impression of past and future, when, in truth, neither exist. The past is a moment gone from existence and the future is a moment yet to exist. If we were to take away these illusions of past and future we are left with the unknown, emptiness, the experience of the present moment here and now.

Neuroscientists would also add that our neurons work in synchronicity like a chain reaction. One neuron fires to stimulate another, which stimulates another and so on. They suggest that this provides us with a sensation of time passing.

So, there is a distinction between subjective time - the time we experience relative to our movement in comparison to other objects - and objective time - which is the time we have created by dividing the earth's rotation around the sun into units on a clock. But neither truly exist, they are mind-made and man-made concepts imbedded within our psyche.

Time is not a steady constant and in fact, it does not truly exist. The only thing we can conclude is that the present moment, here and now, is the only true constant.

"The present moment helps us recognise the minds empty nature and the illusion of phenomenon"

His Holiness the Dali Lama

WHAT IS REAL ANYWAY?

As with every weekday morning, my bed room door opened ajar as my mother peeks into my room to softy tell me the time:

"Anthony, it's 7:30am"

I must have been about twelve or thirteen years old and my mother's wakeup call worked perfectly well apart from one occasion.

I remember this instance well because, each time I was woken by my mother's voice I must have fallen back to sleep and dreamt that I had gotten up. On the first occasion, I dreamt I had brushed my teeth, packed my bag and put on my school uniform.

"Anthony, it's 7:45. Time to get up"

I recall being surprised and amused. I genuinely believed I was out of bed and getting ready. However, without realising it, once again, I fell back to sleep, dreaming that I was fully dressed and eating my breakfast cereal in the kitchen.

The door opened: *"Anthony, it's nearly 8 o'clock! Get up!"*

Waking with a start my mind scrambled to reconcile the belief that I had been up for a while and was enjoying my breakfast downstairs with the reality of finding myself still in bed. Nevertheless, I fell straight back to sleep a fourth time, dreaming I was on now my bike and almost at school. Just as each dream before, every detail of my morning routine was perfectly real to me.

To my mother's utter exasperation on waking me a fourth time and despite my earnest protest that I believed I had acted to my mother's commands, the cold wet flannel to my feet ensured there was no falling back to sleep a fifth time.

I remember this because it was such a strange experience. Each dream was so real to me. I was absolutely convinced I had risen from beneath my duvet and was genuinely on my way to school. Because I was so convinced that my dreams were my reality I began to ask myself questions.

How would I know if I was dreaming or awake? After all, both a dream and waking experiences occur in the mind. Both experiences involve firing neurons in the brain to create images, sensations and experiences. It would be more accurate to state reality as an interpretation rather than a direct and accurate experience.

Could what we see and experience be false? After all, there is a myriad of spectrums known to be unseen to our eyes such as radio, infrared, ultraviolet, X-ray and gamma-rays. Astronomers can get more information about stars and other distant cosmic phenomena by using instruments which detect these different types of "invisible" light. As it is our own mind which interprets the information entering our senses, how can we honestly know for certain what reality is?

Is the common reality we interact with each day how things are? Could our minds be misinterpreting information? Can we truly trust what we see, hear and feel?

Philosopher Lazarus Geiger (1829 - 1870) analysed ancient Icelandic, Hindu, Chinese, Arabic and Hebrew texts to find no mention of the word blue so he theorized that they perhaps were unable to see the colour. Many years later Jules Davidoff, a psychologist from Goldsmiths University of London, found that the Himba tribe from Namibia had no word to describe the colour blue either and sure enough, the tribal members were unable to distinguish a blue object amongst other colours suggesting they could not see it. Conversely, native Russian speakers, who have several words for blue can discriminate between light and dark shades of blue much faster than English speakers. This suggests that until we had a word for blue it was unlikely to exist for our ancestors. Or, more accurately, they could not perceive it.

When admiring a beautiful brightly coloured rose, the lush green grass of a meadow or a glassy turquoise ocean, the reality is, the colours you observe are, in fact, not there.

Of course, conventionally, we see the different colours, so it exists in that sense but in true reality nothing has colour. The sun omits white light which is composed of various light waves with different lengths and frequencies which we can see when refracted through rain droplets to project primary colours within a rainbow. Depending on the physical qualities of an object, light waves will be absorbed or reflected. Those waves which are reflected are interpreted via our eyes and brain to assign the colour we see.

If we took away our mind and its interpretations, what would the real world look like?

When in deep dreaming sleep, we are unaware of our unconscious state, so it follows that when 'conscious' how can we know we are not still dreaming? All interactions with the outside world from the things we touch, smell, hear and taste are merely electrical interpretations of the mind. Like images on our Tv screens are interpretations of digital signals transferred via electrical cables, our brain works similarly.

Such philosophical questions have been debated for years and, while I am not suggesting that we are part of a computer program - although some scientists would suggest that it is not such an absurd idea - advances in scientific research informs us that what we experience as reality is not at all how things really are.

In comparison to other animals, you have the unique advantage of analytical thought to investigate and delve deep into the very fabric of our existence. As our reality is formed from decoded and interpreted sensory information by the mind, it seems logical that we should use the mind to help recognise its tricks, misinterpretations, delusions and false perceptions of reality. If we can comprehend the falsities of the mind, begin to understand the true nature of ourselves and reality, we can begin to peel back the illusions and observe a completely different world, the first world reality.

If you have read one of my other books, such as, *What's the Point? A Guild to Life and Happiness,* or listened to one of my audiobooks via the website (wisemonkeytraining.co.uk), then you may have heard me talk about the quantum world before. To save repeating myself, and avoid labouring the fact, I will cut straight to the heart of this chapter.

Newtonian physics states that the physical and material world consists of separate entities which influence one another. Traditional biology would claim something very similar, stating that our body consists of parts which are individual and separate from each other.

This notion suggests that our body and the physical world outside of us comprises of separate individual parts which, when put together, work as a single unit. Much like a car engine, the battery is separate to the pistons which, in turn are separate from the cambelt and so forth. Although they are working together to form the engine, the engine itself is not a unified, holistic object. The spark plug can be replaced without effecting the rest of the component parts of the engine, much like traditional biology would believe a human heart can be removed and replaced without effecting the overall function of other body parts.

Quantum physics changed this view. In the quantum world everything is one unified and holistic field of energy which is incontestably connected and intertwined.

It all started with the discovery that all matter was made of atoms. With advancements in technology we could delve deeper to find the structure of atoms consisted of protons and neutrons. Looking further still we find protons and neutrons were made of quarks, which are not solid particles but in fact waves of energy.

If we then work backwards from quarks to form atoms, molecules and physical matter, we can understand that everything in the entire universe is made of energy. This single, unified field of energy is the first world view, the true reality and the ultimate truth about how things really exist.

The irony of course is that waves of energy are not physical in the sense that they can be touched so, in true reality, nothing exists physically as our minds would have us believe.

This is the Buddhist concept of emptiness which is the true nature of things. Of course, the second world view exists theoretically as a concept and fabrication of our mind. We can continue to interact with it, engage with it, play within it and enjoy it but there is another reality which exists, the first world view, the true reality of unified energy, oneness and ultimate connection with all things. Once we can access the first world we can dramatically influence and transform the second world. This is where we move from mind over matter to mind over mind for it is our mind which creates and observes the second world view and therefore, our mind which can 'unobserve' it to unveil the first world reality.

For our mind, which has been wired and conditioned to perceive a separate and solid second world, this can be an extremely hard concept to fully comprehend. The only way to truly understand and view this ultimate truth is through the door of the present moment. Within the present moment time ceases to exist and without time the physical world can no longer exist to our mind because the physical second world objects can only be experienced through thought and thoughts manifest in past and future. i.e. time.

Elimination of time causes the elimination of second world objects and allows access to the first world reality.

For example, as you read this book you might say, I am holding this book thus, instinctively referring to the action in the past tense. We could say, I hold the book, which would be present tense, but this would not technically be correct because only after the action has occurred can you say that it has happened. Only after picking the book up can you state that you hold it but, of course, at this point you are holding it. In this way we can begin to recognise that our interaction with the physical can only be processed after the interaction itself. Also, all exchanges with the material world must be processed via the brain first in order for us to interpret it and then experience it. This means nothing we do physically can truly transpire in the present moment and is entirely reliant on the mind-made concept of time.

Likewise, you cannot experience and comprehend a sentence within this book without reading each word first. The passage of time is necessary for you to experience this physical second world object. It would be impossible to read this page without the passage of time. If you were able to eliminate time, the words would not be cognized.

Even the table we see in front of us is not existing in the present moment. The light reflected off its surface travels through space to reach our eyes, the photons travel through the intraocular fluid before hitting our retinas which sends a signal to the brain via the optic nerves which must be interpreted before relaying information back out, so we can see the table. Agreed, this entire process happens in a fraction of a second, but it still relies upon time which is not existent in the present moment.

Remember, even the colour of the table – or anything else for that matter - is not a truth about its existence. Different materials absorb different wave lengths whilst reflecting others. Those which are reflected reach our eyes and are interpreted as a particular colour. Therefore, the grass is not green but merely seen as green due to the consistency of each blade which reflects certain light frequencies whilst absorbing all others. So, what is the true colour of grass? Does it have a colour at all?

Physical objects only exist as a by-product of our interaction with them, and our experience of this second world is entirely reliant on thought and thought is entirely reliant on time, which, once again, does not inherently exist in true reality.

Connected and engrossed within the present moment we lose concept of time, thoughts therefore cannot be and the physical world – which includes our own body – cease to exist. In this realm, the ultimate truth can be discovered and experienced. Without the existences of our physical body we are left with our consciousness. Like plugging our computer into the internet, it is through the present moment that we can connect with all things and this is when the fun and magic really starts to happen.

CONSCIOUSNESS

When we think of consciousness we tend to think of being awake and thinking, however, consciousness is more than simply not being asleep and nor is it confined to be brain. Neuroscientists will measure brain function and structure to explain consciousness, but the real challenge is to investigate consciousness subjectively through human experience. Objective study of consciousness involves the left, rational and thinking side of the of the brain whilst subject experience of consciousness, via meditation for example, involves the right, intuitive and feeling side of the brain.

Previously, we briefly discussed the pitfalls of attachment and that we should avoid mental attachment to the material and physical second world. Perhaps you can begin to appreciate the necessity for non-attachment because it keeps us stuck within the realm of our second world and prevents us from entering the present moment. With thoughts strongly attached to the material world outside of the present moment our mind remains connected to all physical objects within the second world and to the concept of time. With a strong attachment to these things it is impossible to be present within the here and now and therefore, impossible to experience the ultimate truth of first world reality.

If you fully understand what it means to release mental focus and attachment from the illusory second world, you may – conceptually at least – feel at ease with letting go of your material possessions but one thing may remain ensnared to your mind and that is the conception of yourself.

When you become embarrassed or feel strong emotions, your concept of self feels physical. In this context the idea that 'I' am being affected seems very real when in fact 'I' only exists as a concept of your mind.

In the scientific community the 'I' is referred to as the 'Observer' – the conscious entity which seems to reside within us and can observe internal emotions and thoughts.

To help release attachment from the concept that you exist as a separate, individual, physical being, it helps to regularly sit in silence and work through the following analytical thought process:

Sit quietly and notice your thoughts. Notice the 'I' observing your thoughts. Conclusion: The 'I' therefore is not your thoughts because it is able to view your thoughts as a separate entity from it.

Notice that you naturally refer to your mind as "My mind", as if the mind is a possession of the 'I' and your mind belongs to 'I'. We therefore instinctively understand that the mind is not the 'I' and the 'I' is something separate from it. Your mind also has varying states of awareness (when asleep, in a trance-like meditative state and fully awake for example) and yet your 'I' remains a separate constant and unchanged entity. Conclusion: The 'I' is not your mind.

We say the same about our body parts such as "My Leg" or "My arm" so, once again, we inherently refer to the 'I' as something separate from our body and its parts. Also, we can lose many parts of our body and the 'I' still remains unchanged. Conclusion: The 'I' is not the body or its parts.

Is the 'I' an amalgamation of body and mind? Having established that the 'I' is neither body or mind, it is impossible for them to become 'I' in combination. Two things which are not an experience cannot become an experience together. Conclusion: The 'I' is not a combination of body and mind.

So, what are you left with? Conclusion: Nothing or as Buddhists call it, Emptiness.

Going through this thought experiment to discover the non-existence of self can help us recognise our true nature and the nature of consciousness. The thing which causes you to feel as if negative emotions are affecting you does not exist. The thing we think is being affected by events and circumstances does not exist inherently. Again, you do exist conceptually of course but not in true first world reality.

The first law of thermodynamics states that energy cannot be created or destroyed but moves from one form to another. Perhaps when we pass from this life it is merely a transfer of energy and it is only our attachment to the second world – which includes ourselves - which makes it feel fearful? After the death of Einstein's dear friend Michelle Besso in 1955 he was quoted saying:

"Now he has departed from this strange world a little ahead of me. That means nothing. People like us, who believe in physics, know that the distinction between past, present and future is only a stubbornly persistent illusion"

In 2007, John Updegraff and colleague Eunkook Suh published a research paper in the Journal of Positive Psychology which suggests people with a more abstract concept of themselves (i.e. as energy or universal consciousness) are happier in comparison to those who view 'I' as a 'solid', separate and physical object.

Moreover, if we continue to use this same reasoning towards all objects we can come to the same conclusion which is that all things exist as conceptual constructs of the mind to form the second world. In first world reality however, we know that the true nature of things is emptiness, or rather, consciousness. This concept is supported by quantum physics because when a physical object is broken down into its parts we find that these parts are not the object we perceive. In fact, the very foundation of objects at the atomic level are vast 'gaps' of space rather than condense solid matter. In 1910, Earnest Rutherford fired charged particles towards gold sheets and found that only 0.01 percent of these particles bounced back. The conclusion he uncomfortably had to accept – and was later confirmed – was that particles are vastly more empty space than solid matter. Even so, when the solid parts of atoms are broken down we find that they are waves of energy and not solid at all. A million atoms are no more solid than just one and so, if the fabric of all things is non-solid energy then how can the anything be solid in truth?

In conclusion, we find that ourselves, and all things, are not solid as our minds would have us believe but in fact, without our consciousness there is no object but rather a unified field of energy. Thus, in first world reality there is no separation between yourself and all things throughout the entire universe. To unveil this magical first world we must enter through the door via the present moment.

This is supported further by numerous studies into the benefits of meditation which shows regular meditators gain an increased sense of oneness and connection (which we will cover in detail later). In contrast, non-meditators tend to hold a more separate and divided view of themselves.

From studies of meditation we know that the brain can become more organised and holistic through concentrated focus of attention. The theta and gamma wave signals from the brain become coherent, magnified and stronger. We also know that meditation stimulates cognitive growth and shown to significantly decrease cognitive decline in older adults as a result.

We know that meditation is a means to become unified within the present moment allowing the coherent signal of the brain to transmit conscious intention information with increased effectiveness. These special qualities and abilities gained via meditation can influence the second world reality and heal oneself and others.

On request, healers have long been unofficially used to support cancer patients and specialist's psychologist Lawrence LeShan has identified two key elements of such healers. The first is for them to attain an altered state of consciousness via meditation and the second is to lose identity of self, to lose attachment to the concept of 'I' and connect with the patient as one.

In my book, *The Business Plan for Happiness*, I discuss evidence-based techniques to help rewire the mind and attain more happiness. Interestingly, studies of positivity, show one of the effects of developing a more positive mind to be the decrease of self-conception. Via the practice of positivity, whereby you put effort into rewiring your cognitive filters to view second world reality more optimistically, the mental concept of "me" being separate from "you" and "us" being separate from "them", decreases. Through the effort of paying attention to positive thoughts in favour of negative thoughts we can adjust our neural network to develop an expansion of mind and body which seems to have the added effect of lessening the ego to become less separate and more unified. With a more positive and less egotistic perception, new possibilities for connection emerge.

"With positivity, you go from classifying people as separate to seeing more interconnection, as "we" and "us". The effect is so reliable that we've found it cross-culturally"

Dr Barbara Fredrickson in Positivity

In Buddhist scriptures, consciousness is rather beautifully defined as that which is luminous and knowing. In other words, consciousness provides us with the mental ability to luminate our own thoughts, to observe and analyse our thoughts.

Consciousness allows us to know or perceive both the second and first worlds.

If consciousness is the entity which sheds light on our own mind and allows us to apprehend the physical and metaphysical world then we can conclude that it is a separate entity, independent of mind, body and matter. However, without consciousness neither mind, body or matter would exist. <u>Consciousness is the creator of reality, it must be present for things to come into existence.</u>

I encourage you to reflect on this last statement because you are masters of your consciousness, you choose where to direct it and therefore what to bring into existence. It is important to begin to identify that you are not a passive observer of reality, you are co-creator.

"The World is not there...it is not independent of consciousness. Quantum science is very clear about that"

Amit Goswami. University of Oregon Institute of Theoretical Physics.

The very nature of viewing ourselves as a separate entity from everything and everyone else creates divide between "us" and "them", "here" and "there", "coming" and "going", "being" and "not being", "one" and "many", "beginning" and "end". On the other hand, without an independent and individualised view of oneself we see sameness, equality, inclusion, connection and unity.

CO-CREATOR

As with time, the physical second world reality cannot be denied but is relative to our mind and its cognitive filters. All things observed are co-dependent on the mind, nothing appears without the presence of a conscious mind and therefore all things come into existence through the interaction of consciousness and matter. Nothing exists independently from the mind and thus, we can conclude that all things are connected.

It was this logical progression of thought which brought Einstein, Boris Podolsky and Nathan Rosen together in 1935. Long debates continued into the early hours for many days. Mathematic equations were shared and ideas deliberated at length. In the end they could not escape the real possibility that reality could consist of non-solid waves of energy and this energy could pop into existence as particles when observed by conscious attention. Prior to conscious intervention physical matter exists nowhere and everywhere at the same time. Despite their attempts to prove the contrary, they could not escape the figures on paper which continually suggested that this was indeed the case.

This mastermind group, of arguably the greatest minds in history, continued to consider the implications of their findings. If reality were indeed constructed of energy, then there would be no boundaries between one thing and another, all things throughout the entire universe would be connected. Furthermore, if all things are connected then information could be communicated from one place to another regardless of space or time.

In other words, if all things are energy then all things are connected and if this were so, then an action over 'here' would influence an object over 'there'. All matter would be entangled.

It was not until 1998 that Nicolas Gisin confirmed Einstein, Podolsky and Rosen's calculations. Gisin's experiment involved sending two photons separated from the same source of light in opposite directions along an optical fibre. At each end of the optical tube were junction points, one going left and the other going right. The distance between one junction at one end and the opposition junction at the other end of the cable was six miles.

Gisin wanted to test Einstein, Podolsky and Rosen's thought experiment and see if one photon was connected to the other, irrespective of time or distance. If this were true, then at the end of the optical fibre when one photon went left at the junction the other would also go left, and if one went right the other would go right.

This is exactly what happened. Time and time again, without fail, each photon mimicked the behaviour of the other every time. Additionally, this happened instantly even though each photon was six miles apart.

This experiment and many others like it have been replicated to reliably produce the same outcome. Furthermore, as investigations into this bizarre phenomenon continued, it became apparent that consciousness influenced what was observed.

The Double-slit experiment has become rather infamous and widely used as an example of the influence of consciousness on reality, so I will avoid discussing it in detail and provide a summary for those who may not have come across it.

To identify if an electron was a solid particle or a wave of energy, an experiment was set up to settle the matter. The concept was simple and involved sending a single electron towards a plate containing two vertical slits at its centre. If electrons were indeed solid, the individual particles would travel through a slit and over time form an imprint of the two slits on a sheet behind the plate.

The strangeness started when the imprint on the back sheet did not show two vertical lines as expected but instead an interference wave pattern. The electron was a wave not a particle.

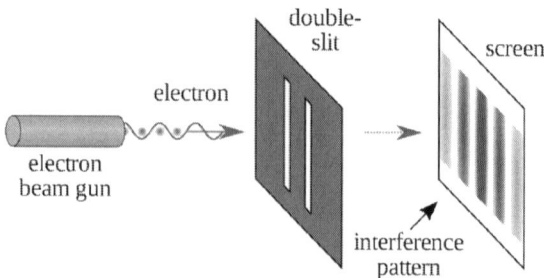

The scientist then set up an observation device outside the slits, so they could witness what was happening. Once set up the experiment was run again but this time the electron behaved as a solid particle marking the back sheet with two vertical lines.

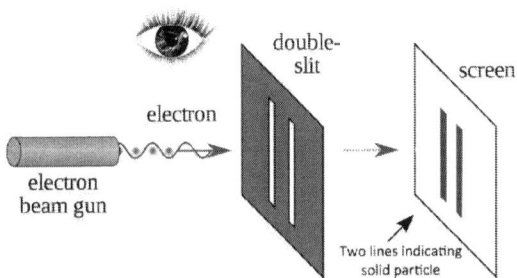

This was the first of numerous experiments which continued to show the same results. When unobserved the foundational elements of matter were waves of energy but when observed it turned into solid particles.

These experiments left the physics community with a highly controversial yet undeniable conclusion:

- The addition of consciousness (observation) causes waves to turn into particles.

In summary, these experiments show that the mere act of looking at a foundational element of matter makes it behave as if it were a solid, physical particle. We effectively bring that matter into existence. Without the presence of consciousness, the element remains in its natural state as a wave of energy.

Moreover, left without the addition of consciousness, these waves of energy (which, do not forget, is the elemental substance of all physical matter) exists in all places and all positions. A single wave function is everywhere and nowhere at the same time and appears where we look for it.

Think of an arrow shot from an archers' bow. The arrow is flying through the air but we cannot determine its position unless we stop it in one place. Therefore, the position we find it is the place where we stop its flight. But without stopping the arrow we are unable to state its position in space and time, in fact, at that moment it could be anywhere. This is like the conundrum presented with foundational elements of matter. When we observe the particle it appears in a fixed location as a physical object but up until that point it is everywhere as energy.

You are not a passive observer of reality, you are co-creator.

"It is not possible to formulate the laws of physics in a fully consistent way without reference to the consciousness of the observer"

Physicist, Eugene Wigner

Another way to help explain the issue of seeing first world reality from a second world perspective is to look at the image above.

Your mind may perceive the faces and then 'flick' to make the vase appear but you cannot view both at the same time. To view the faces is to not perceive the vase and to view the vase is to not perceive the faces. Equally, the black shape of the vase would not exist without the white of shape of the faces and therefore, neither would exist without the presence of the other and yet, both cannot be perceived at the same time. They co-exist interdependently.

If we were to completely erase the black vase from the image, the faces would cease to exist. The opposite is also true. If we assume the white faces are upon a black background, when removed, the vase would also disappear.

Similarly, if we were to remove the physical second world, the unified field of first world reality would not exist. Likewise, if we were to remove the first world reality, the physical second world would not exist.

It is necessary for us to be born as conscious beings to observe the second world view and discover the first world view. This is the meaning of life; to find, experience and access the hidden wonders of the first world reality to see the vase when previously we could only see the faces. To not use this precious life to access this first world reality is to live in ignorance or, as the great philosopher Alan Watts says, to live in "ignore-ance".

One variation of the 'six-mile optical fibre' experiment combined the witnessing of entanglement with the effect of conscious viewing.

The instruments were arranged in a very similar way as before but this time at each end of the optic fibre was placed a double- slit plate rather than a junction. At one end only was added a viewing device so the experimenters could 'watch' the electron as it approached the double-slits.

From the original double-slit tests, the scientists knew that the act of 'watching' would cause the collapse of wave function and it would enter through the slits as a particle rather than a wave of energy.

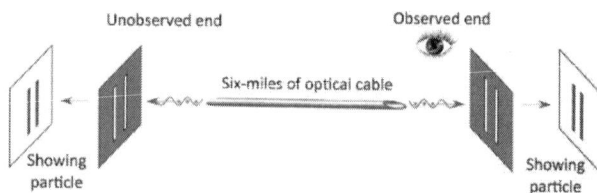

What they found further confirmed entanglement, or, "spooky action at a distance" as Einstein called it. If the observation device was used then, as expected, the electron behaved as a particle, however, so did the electron at the other end of the fibre. If the viewing equipment was not used both electrons remained as energy waves. It was clear that, despite great distances, one electron knew what was happening to the other, instantaneously.

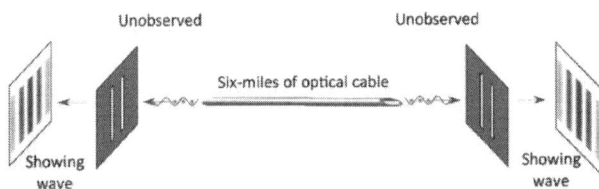

Not only are we co-creators of the second world reality we see, feel and interact with, the first world reality consists of a single, unified energy source which communicates instantly across any distance.

This entanglement of matter affirms that past and future are illusions of mind. We are conditioned and programmed to think that what I do here cannot instantaneously influence something elsewhere without being local to it and exerting physical force against it. And yet, many experiments confirm that time and space is not a truth in first world reality.

"Objects do not exist intrinsically at all. But this is not to say they do not exist. The entities that we identify exist in relation to us and they perform the function that we attribute to them. But their very existence as we define them, is dependent upon our verbal and conceptual designation"

Alan Wallace

Like the discussions had in 1935 with Einstein, Podolsky and Rosen, astrophysicists Trinh Xuan Thuan, from the University of Virginia, and Buddhist Monk Matthieu Ricard debated the topic of consciousness and entanglement. The scientist and the Monk agree that nothing is independent but rather interdependent with consciousness. The physical reality we experience each day through our senses is the effect caused by consciousness and therefore, without this cause the objects and matter we interact with would not exist. Because we are conscious beings, it is we who bring reality into existence, we cannot say that matter does not exist, but neither can we state that it exists independently of our mind.

Armed with this information, what can we say about consciousness?

- As consciousness is necessary for the existence of matter within the second world reality, we can say confidently that it extends beyond the physical boundaries of our body.

- Consciousness brings order to the second world reality by causing the collapse of energy, so we can touch, feel and interact within objects, people and materials. Without consciousness there would be no order or structure to the material second world.

- The strength of consciousness is directly proportionate to the order observed within the second world view. This relates to our neurological structure which is formed by our own thoughts, emotions and behaviours as already discussed. It also relates to the fact that where our attention goes our energy flows, so if our attention is erratic, leaping stressfully from one thing to another, then it stands to reason that our second world will appear as chaotic and disorganised. Moreover, this point also relates to forming mental focus to produce mind-body coherence (which we will discuss in more detail shortly).

- Several coherent (intentionally focused) minds magnify the influence of consciousness upon the second world reality. We know this from group meditation sessions which have demonstrated remarkable impacts on the second world such as reduced crime rates and drastic improvements in sick individuals.

- A group of experienced meditators were asked to focus their minds with the intention of reducing crime within New York City on a specific day. On that day crime rates plummeted to lowest levels in years and went back up the following day.

- In another experiment a group of people were asked to wish an unwell individual recovery. At first this did nothing to improve health. Undeterred the experimenters refined the experiment and repeated it but this time with very specific instructions so that all were focusing on a very specific intended outcome. The result dramatically improved health within targeted individuals.

- Physical systems respond to consciousness by becoming more ordered. In a seemingly chaotic second world reality where we juggle so many daily hassles, chores and stressors, it may be hard to believe that we have the power to bring order to our lives through the development of a more coherent mind.

Through scientific investigation a clear picture of reality is being formed. No longer can we say that the physical world exists independently from our consciousness, in fact, we can, with confidence, now state that it is consciousness which manifests the material second world view.

Only via our own conscious attention is the cause in place for potential to become actual. Only via the cause of conscious intention can we observe the effect.

Hopefully, now you have a clearer understanding of the two worlds. The second world of physical matter is the conventional truth which is conceptually real to the mind but is not inherently real and does not exist without a conscious mind. Whereas the first world reality is the ultimate truth and consists of a connected, communicating, unified field of energy and therefore, its ultimate nature is "emptiness".

It is poignant to note that seventy-four percent of the universe is thought to be an invisible energy called dark energy and twenty-two percent is thought to be dark matter, neither of which are currently measurable. In other words, *ninety-six* percent of the universe is unknown energy.

At the conventional level of second world reality, matter abides by rules and physical laws of Newtonian physics, but these rules fall away the instant we access the first world reality.

Seeing objects as separate, traditional science looks to see how inanimate matter caused the origin of sentient beings whereas Buddhist philosophy investigates how sentient beings cause the origins of matter. Buddhist philosophy holds that all matter, including ourselves, are energy and for matter to become sentient, it must contain consciousness. Quantum physics would agree with this view.

CHAPTER 13

INFLUENCING REALITY

This is all very well in the micro subatomic world of photons, electrons and quarks but can we really apply the phenomenon of entanglement to the macro second world, in which we live?

This is the question now being asked as scientists scale up experiments to find out if 'spooky action at a distance' occurs between larger objects too. In other words, can larger physical objects communicate and instantly 'know' what the other is doing across vast distances? Can an object large enough to be seen with the naked eye influence another across space?

Unsurprisingly, to test entanglement with larger objects is a complicated business but it has been carried out with DNA, molecules and bacteria to produce the same results. Objects which have been in contact are intertwined and connected. Each 'knows' what the other is doing and therefore can influence each other. Again, this connection is non-local and can be seen at any distance and there is no delay in the communication between the two sister objects. The two objects behave as if they are one.

The problem with testing entanglement in larger objects is the fact that they must originate from the same source or be tangled before being separated but Huping Hu (now President at QuantumDream Inc.) and his colleague Maxoxin Wu, had an idea. They passed a magnetic pulse through an anaesthetic solution before passing the same magnetic energy onto a patient. The idea being that the magnetic energy mixes and connects with the atomic energy within the aesthetic substance thus, becomes entangled, causing the numbing action of the anaesthetic to be felt by the patient when the magnetic pulse as passed through them. And it worked.

They even took it a step further by passing the painkilling infused magnetic field through water and asked the patient to drink it. Once again, the anaesthesia took effect.

The implications of this for the evolution of humanity and human experience is immense and consequently has given more credibility to noetic science.

Noetic originates from the Greek word noesis, meaning direct inner knowing. Scientific research in this area includes psychic phenomena such as mind-to-mind communication, (telepathy), the ability to see distant objects or events (clairvoyance), the ability to see future events (precognition) and mind-matter interactions (psychokinesis). Noetic scientific endeavour aims to find evidence of entanglement within human beings.

A study of identical twins, who of course are formed from the same egg, would be a good place to start this investigation. One of the first experiments was published in 1965 in the journal of science. The test involved measuring brain waves and activity within identical twins. Separated in separate rooms, one twin was exposed to certain stimulus which were known to either activate a specific area of the brain or cause measurable changes in brain waves. Sure enough, throughout each experiment with numerous sets of twins the data clearly showed that changes in one siblings brain instantly evoke matching changes in the other.

This type of experiment and variations of it have been repeated countless times over the years since and the results are always the same.

If this type of mind and matter connection can occur in twins, what about between the rest of us, between one human to another?

You might be sceptical about such studies, especially if you consider the fact that entanglement only works between two objects which have been previously intimately connected. However, we forget that we are all from the same source, we, and in fact the entire universe, were once intricately conjoined at the point of the Big Bang. We are all made of the same matter from the very same original source.

It is known from studies that when seeing someone being inflicted with pain, pain receptors within the viewers brain light up like a Christmas Tree. We know that female menstrual cycles become synchronised when living together. The concept is therefore not new to us and yet, we rarely stand back and wonder at its implications.

Experiments involving couples (e.g. Husband and Wife) separated by 'sealed' and insulated rooms show similar entangled minds. One of the couple was asked to "send" certain emotions to their partner. To help create the requested emotion, relevant images where shown (e.g. happy images, sad images and neutral (non-emotional stimulating images).

The partner receiving the emotions in another room was wired to an EGG (Electrogastrogram) which measures gut activity. When highly emotional states were sent, the receiving partner measured higher gut activity when compared to neutral or non-emotional images.

This experiment was run with twenty-six couples and statistical analysis showed the chances of the result being a coincidence or a fluke, is very low indeed.

In another experiment couples were asked to mentally "send" a given image (e.g. a picture of an animal, building or object) to their partner who was 'receiving' the image in another sealed room. After a measured "sending" period, the 'receiver' is offered four unrelated images and asked to choose the one which was thought to be sent by their partner in the other room. When the results of all such experiments were collected and combined, the chances against the positive results being down to chance or luck were odds of 517 to 1.

To put these odds another way, imagine having a sealed opaque bag of marbles, all of which are blue apart from one which is red. Before you delve your hand blindly into the bag you focus your mind and intend to pick the red marble amongst the blues and you are successful five-hundred and sixteen times out of five-hundred and seventeen attempts. In this scenario you would have to conclude that the odds are too great to assign to coincidence or accident.

Another experiment was so simple it became widely replicated. In this test, a participant was given a predetermined number between one and six and asked to focus their attention on that number to influence the way a tossed dice landed. To help eliminate any human bias, the dice were tossed by a machine whilst the individual mentally intended for it to settle in such a way that their chosen number faced upwards. The results showed a person's wish for a dice to land with a specific number facing upwards was statistically significant.

Because it was relatively easy to replicate, scientists across the world ran the dice intention experiment for themselves which meant more data. Dr Dean Radin and his team, at the Institute of Noetic

Sciences in California, decided to accumulate the results from all these studies to provide larger statistical 'weight'. After eliminating those which did not meet scientific standards, Dr Radin was left with seventy-three relevant studies, involving some two thousand five-hundred people. When combined, the collated results showed the chances of the positive correlations being pure luck were 1096 to 1.

To put this into some perspective, imagine you throw a dice 1096 times, and with each throw you focus your mental attention to intend the dice to land with your chosen number facing up.

10,00000000000000000000000000000000000000 00000000000000000000000000000000000000000 0000000000000000 throws later, only one did not land with the intended number facing upwards. It would be more unbelievable to suggest that this was just a fluke or pure luck. With such odds against chance, it would seem certain that something very real was happening between mental intention and the behaviour of the dice.

So, your conscious intentions can not only connect with other people but also with inanimate objects too.

Dean Radin has published the results of numerous experiments investigating the ability of consciousness to influence other objects in scientific journals and books such as, *Entangled Minds* and *The Conscious Universe*. As a scientist, Radin is critical of experiments to ensure they achieve valid results attained via rigorous research standards. Many trials which meet these criteria are seen to produce positive results with odds of millions-to-one chance of being caused by fluke or luck.

As entanglement moved from a mathematical possibility to a scientifically accepted fact, even hardened sceptics of noetic studies opened their minds to take notice. The bioentanglement – quantum connection between living things explains holistic qualities and properties in nature.

After review of evidence, in 1981 the Congressional Research Service agreed that studies in parapsychology and noetic science show an interconnectedness between mind and matter.

"The interconnectedness would appear to be functional in nature and amplified by intent and emotion"

U.S. Library of Congress 1983.

Two things are abundantly clear:

1. The concept of you being separate from everything around you is an illusion.
2. Your conscious intention has the power to directly influence your internal and external environment. The idea that you have little or no influence on your current or future life is also a misapprehension. Of course, you can physically make changes to influence your life outcomes, but evidence now strongly suggests that the real power lies in your conscious intentions.

Through intention, belief and associated emotion you connect to this powerful facet of reality and influence matter. It follows therefore, that if the message your consciousness is 'sending' out is one of hopelessness, limited control and worry, for example, then this message is 'received' by all people and all things around you which can, and will, change your reality to match.

"Physicists now believe that entanglement between particles exists everywhere, all the time, and have recently found shocking evidence that it affects the wider, 'macroscopic' world that we inhabit"

Michael Brooks, New Scientist magazine, 2004

Thoughts, beliefs and intentions are being broadcast outwardly and inwardly. This message reverberates across the universal field instantaneously communicating and influencing matter and reality to align with your message.

Similarly, you are picking up on the signals sent from others too. This constant and immediate communication between all things shapes, cultivates and manifests. Your consciousness is one and the same as that which connects all things. This can be represented by the water in a lake. When you send out a conscious message a ripple radiates outwards. The lake is the first world reality, the universal field of energy, in fact, many now refer to this fabric of reality as *The Field*.

As scientists are unable to find where in the mind memory is formed and stored, it is now proposed that The Field holds conscious information and thus, our memories.

If information is being endlessly passed round The Field, could it be possible that information could be stored there too? If so, could it also be true to suggest that, as we are all energy and therefore receiving the information and memories of all sentient beings, we can learn and develop from the collective memory within The Field?

In other words, thoughts are known to be transmitted instantly within The Field and influence physical matter, including ourselves. Therefore, could it be possible that we are evolving and learning via The Field also?

"Entanglement would lead to a Darwinian advantage. It could coordinate biochemical reactions in different parts of the cell, or in different parts of an organ. It could allow correlated firings of distant neurons and coordinate the behaviour of members of species"

Physicist Johann Summhammer

In the early 1950's, primatologists were studying Japanese macaques. To enable the researchers to study these monkeys in the open they left food on the beach causing the monkeys to climb down from the trees onto the beach to gather the fruit. After a few weeks, one of the senior monkeys began washing the sand off the fruit in the ocean. Learning by example, gradually, over time, other monkeys copied her. However, when the hundredth monkey began washing its fruit, suddenly all monkeys instantly picked up the habit as if the learned behaviour had reached some critical point of conscious knowledge.

This was interesting, but the real extraordinary fact was only discovered later when a separate group of scientists studying a completely detached tribe of monkeys on a neighbouring island reported a sudden, on mass, behaviour change of washing fruit in the shallows. This instant and collective change in behaviour happened on the very same day.

The new behaviour of washing food appeared to be transmitted to all monkeys of this species instantly across hundreds of miles. Some form of group consciousness had occurred. As is typical with such unexplained phenomena at that time, it was not widely published for fear of ridicule and therefore went mostly unreported until Lyall Watson found the brief notations within the reports and called it, The Hundredth Monkey Phenomena.

It is now proposed that this phenomenon explains the sudden and collective migration of birds. It is interesting to note that even those of new generations or birds raised and released from rescue centres 'know' their migration ritual, even if they have not witnessed it. The same could be said for the collective relocation of spawning salmon and other such sudden shared ceremonial activities within the animal kingdom.

This collective learning from the memory of universal consciousness has since been studied and called Morphic Resonance (pioneered by Dr Rupert Sheldrake) which refers to the collective memory of The Field from which we can learn.

If we too are evolving, learning and developing from each other via The Field of consciousness, we would see an improvement in the standardized IQ test, which is proven to be the case. Our ability to recognise actual words amongst invented words within unlearned languages is also true. For instance, when presented with a list of actual Chinese words amongst a mix of Chinese letters with no meaning, even if we have never learnt the language, we are statistically able to identify the real words from the fictional ones. Morphic Resonance would suggest we are taught via The Field from the millions of Chinese nationals. If they know it, at some conscious level, we also know it.

It would also seem that students sitting exams can learn from each other without communicating a single word. In Denmark for example, to prevent cheating, alternate students are given separate parts of an exam paper and, once finished, they are then given the remaining part. Such as, student A is given questions one to six whilst student B is given questions seven to twelve. Once completed, student A is then given questions seven to twelve and student B questions one to six. Morphic Resonance would predict that correct answers in the second part of the exam would be statistically higher when compared to the first part because the mass of students across the country would be sending the answers via The Field. The information will be received (at a deep level of consciousness) by collective examinees allowing them to answer the second section of the exam with more accuracy. Once again, when studied, this turns out to be true.

"The universe exists as a single ocean of intelligence which at its centre is the fountainhead of consciousness and ocean of pure potential and this is what we are"

Professor of Physics John Hagelin

Spiritual leaders have long been suggesting that, as of the year 2012, a conscious shift is occurring which will lead to a new age of enlightened growth within humanity. Perhaps, with the continued freeing of minds from God-based beliefs, allowing investigation of alternatives without fear of damnation, together with advances in science, more people are discovering The Field and this knowledge is being 'picked up' and learnt by the masses via Morphic Resonance.

"I believe we are on the verge of a great evolutionary jump...maybe when we see, remember and awaken to who we truly are, human beings can move as a collective consciousness from a state of survival into a state of thriving"

Dr Joe Dispenza in Becoming Supernatural

DISTURBING THE ENERGY

There are three main ways to disrupt our own energy field and therefore our ability to harmonise and resonate with The Field:

1.   Trauma

2.   Toxins

3.   Thought

Trauma: Trauma can of course come in the form of physical damage to the body or brain, like a dent in the wheel arch of a car which rubs against the tyre, impeding efficiency and function, but trauma can also refer to emotional damage too. The energy flow from a traumatised mind is disrupted and does not flow with ease. Like magnets, crystals also have a natural energy field which, under the guidance of a skilled practitioner, can be used to heal the energy flow. Other energy healers such as Reiki and Emotional Freedom Technique (EFT) practitioners can help to clear blockages or resistance within the energy flow caused by emotional trauma. Neuro-linguistic Programming (NLP), Timeline Therapy™ and Matric Reimprinting are also excellent methods of resolving limiting thoughts, beliefs and behaviours which are preventing mind-body and energy alignment.

The ultimate personal journey follows a common structure as described here. Once we can let go of being a victim we attain understanding and with this understanding we identify feelings of hurt or rejection. Once free from hurt and rejection we notice the guilt and lack of self-esteem. With the attainment of forgiveness for oneself and others we recognise the unfulfilled potential within us. Understanding the nature of mind and universal energy which flows through all things, we can let go of attempts to control the uncontrollable and gain peace, belief and trust that all aspirations and intentions can be achieved. As we further identify the true nature of ourselves and reality, the pressure and responsibility created from labels, duties and roles give way to commitment and focused intention of mind. With this mind state developing we become free from social expectations and can feel deeply contented to simply be who we are. At this point we become a leader of ourselves, our lives and other people will follow. Recognising the power and potential within us can be daunting and yet, with further development of mind, you are able to let go of the fear of power and embrace the infinite found in all things. At this end stage of personal and spiritual growth the last hurdle is to release thoughts of an end to life and truly connect with the oneness of all things. This is the path on which enlightenment can be found.

Toxins: As your body is constantly adjusting internal levels of biochemical and environmental conditions, it follows that an imbalance caused by ingestion of toxins can cause issues with energy flow. A clean healthy eating habit combined with an optimised body from regular exercise enhances the functioning and flow of energy within.

Thoughts: As we now know, the overriding factor to one's ability to align with The Field and thus, our ability to influence, attract and manifest lies within the mind, or more specifically within one's thoughts and beliefs. Where your attention goes energy flows. Sporadic and erratic thoughts which race and leap, are disorganised, uncoordinated and incoherent and thus, so too is the energy.

Like the static on an untuned radio, it is only when your mind and body are tuned into The Field can things be clearly heard.

CHAPTER 14

INCREASING THE ENERGY

The two hemispheres of the brain look identical but have distinct roles. The function of the left hemisphere is largely dedicated to language and self-talk, it processes the detail of information and takes information literally at face-value without interpretation. The right hemisphere on the other hand scopes the bigger picture, processes emotions and the holistic 'feel' of presented information.

The two sides work together to form a picture of the world. Whilst the left allows us to form and write down words using grammatical rules and structure, the right side of the brain enables us to be creative with words to form emotionally evoking passages such as poems, stories and song lyrics, for example. The left hemisphere will identify trees, grass and sky as component parts of a landscape without emotional interpretation, whilst the right hemisphere will absorb the holistic picture to appreciate, admire and feel the beauty of the view.

However, humans have developed a bias towards the left hemisphere creating a highly evolved brain which is dominated by thinking more than feeling. The dominate literal left side of the brain is leaving our emotive right side behind. As a result, we tend to think more than we feel and tend to trust our thoughts over our feelings. This is perhaps the reason why most of us find it hard to meditate because our dominant left, talkative, hemisphere is highly active and prevents us from feeling more. Indeed, one of the main purposes of meditation practice is to reduce mental noise so we can access The Field within the present moment.

We recognise this increased dominance when comparing ourselves to our nearest genetic cousins, the great apes.

The brain is contralateral, meaning the left hemisphere controls the right side of the body and vice versa, the right hemisphere governs the left side of the body. As far as the current research suggests, Apes are equally left-handed or right-handed signifying each side of the brain as likewise prevailing. In contrast, between seventy percent and ninety-five percent of humans are right-handed thus signifying a human bias towards left hemisphere dominance. Interestingly, left-handed people tend to be more creative, intuitive and empathic, again, intimating the holistic, emotional qualities of the right cortex.

As largely governed by our left hemisphere we are more attuned to process the data of information received through our senses and less familiar with our intuitive feelings and gut instincts. As the left hemisphere is predominately developed to use and process language, it is this area which is thought to be largely, if not exclusively, responsible for the internal dialog which chatters constantly within our mind.

When we feel as if we are being watched, for example, our left brain tells us to stop being silly. When we feel like a friend is in need just before we receive a phone call from them asking for help or support, our left brain assigns it to coincidence. When we have a decision to make and cannot decide, we rationalise the choices rather than notice which feels like the right path. When healers can improve a person's clinical condition without touch, our left brain dismisses the results as hokum.

With a dominance of the thinking, chattering, analytical left-brain, it is no wonder we find it hard to focus our energy and direct our intentions accurately.

In my early teens, I would ride home from school at round 3pm. Being a teenager the fifteen-minute journey would often take more like thirty. I would walk through the door, speak with my mother for a while, grab myself a snack and get changed out of my uniform before asking to go out and play with my friends. Dinner was always at 6:30pm during the week so if I made it back promptly in time to eat with the rest of the family I was usually permitted to go out. I would get back on my bike and head back in the direction of school where most of my friends lived. We would play "army" (which was essentially hide and seek but far cooler of course) in the public gardens before one-by-one we all headed back home for dinner. By the time I'd called for friends and started playing I must have had about an hour left, and yet, I distinctly remember feeling like an hour was oodles of time.

Children are very much in the here and now where thoughts of past and future rarely come to mind and the concept of time disappears which is also reflected within their brains too. Children produce mostly alpha and theta waves as they absorb information from experiences directly via the right hemisphere. Adults of course emit mostly beta waves reflecting the dominance of the thinking, mind-chatter of the left hemisphere.

Interestingly, when completely absorbed in an activity, there is very little internal dialog. This 'state of flow' is often described by artists, musicians, dancers and writers who describe it as being freely creative within the moment where time is no longer experienced, and sense of self and environment disappear. Much like a state of trance, a deep feeling of flow transports the individual into the present moment and increases connection to the first world reality where no thought can reside, no effort is noticed, no sense of time exists, surroundings fade and identity with oneself is let go.

Named by Professor Mihály Csikszentmihalyi (pronounced *Me-high Cheek-sent-me-high*), Flow is a mental state of operation in which a person performing an activity is fully immersed in a feeling of energized focus, engaged completely, and enjoyment in the process of the activity. Flow is characterized by complete absorption of consciousness through focused attention.

Csikszentmihalyi identified some fundamentals to enter a state of Flow.

The activity should be on the boundary of your capabilities. If the activity is too easy you will get bored, if it is too hard you will get frustrated. It is the "Goldilocks" state somewhere on the edge of your abilities which is "just right".

The activity should provide immediate feedback. Musicians often find themselves in a state of Flow when they play a challenging piece of music which is complicated but within their ability. The music they can hear being produced from their instrument provides immediate feedback. The same is true with painters and athletes for the same reasons.

Flow state activities should also involve your character strengths which are:

"...positive traits reflected in thoughts, feelings, and behaviours. They exist in degrees and can be measured as individual differences. We speculate that these are grounded in biology through an evolutionary process that selected for these

predispositions toward moral excellence as means of solving the important tasks necessary for survival of the species."

Journal of Social and Clinical Psychology, Vol. 23, No. 5, 2004

In other words, character strengths are a biological bias within you personally which means you naturally enjoy and are attracted to tasks which involve these traits.

There are twenty-four identified character strengths and interestingly studies show kindness, fairness, honesty and gratitude to be the top four across all populations and cultures. Perhaps, most tellingly however is the fact that self-control is universally found to be the lowest strength.

Because of this natural bias, you are likely to find the hobbies and leisure time activities you enjoy will involve your character strengths. This does not necessarily mean you are good at them but nevertheless, they will be activities you seek out and take pleasure in doing.

With a hyperactive left-brain which darts to-and-fro from second world objects, we rarely access this peaceful state of Flow and yet, it is essential for creating a high degree of Morphic Resonance. Within the moment, within the zone where focused intention is highest, the right brain can feel and resonate more freely, and our entire brain becomes coordinated. In a state of Flow the energy frequency within our mind and body becomes coherent and unified.

BECOMING COHERENT

Neuroscience indicates we spend much of our day in a beta brain wave state which can be measured in low, medium and high frequencies. Low-range frequencies occur when we are relaxed but still acutely rooted within the second world where we are conscious of objects and ourselves. Medium-range beta waves occur when we are slightly more stressed, when thinking about a presentation or during an informal interview for example. In this state we are more switched on, imbedded and attached in the second world. Three times higher in comparison to low-range frequency is high-range beta waves which occur when stressed and extremely aware of the external second world because it presents itself as a threat. In this state we are mentally and emotionally invested and attached to the second world as all our attention is directed onto it.

During the day you may drift off into a daydream or imagine yourself back on the beach during a recent holiday. This relaxed state is slightly detached from second world as you become less conscious of it and your brain exhibits alpha brain waves.

As we continue to become less attached to the material second world we enter a theta brain wave state, such as the trance-like state we enter when falling asleep, having a vague awareness of our surroundings, but our mental faculties are largely immersed internally.

Venturing deeper within and moving further away from the second world, such as when dreaming during sleep, we enter delta brain waves and further still into gamma wave frequency.

Beta brain waves can be as high as 40 hertz (cycles per second) whilst gamma waves can be measured as high as 70 hertz. High-range beta waves and gamma waves have the highest frequency, and therefore, energy when compared to other waves. This means when highly stressed our brain is transmitting a high amount of beta wave energy and we become acutely attached to the outer second world. Conversely, when completely detached from the second world, where physical objects, self-concept and time disappear, we are transmitting a lot of theta and gamma energy inwardly providing the body with a vast amount of energy to support healing, rejuvenation and repair.

Coherence occurs when frequencies match and are in synchronization with one another and thus, magnify the intensity of energy. It may come as no surprise to know that an optimally functioning and healthy body has a frequency range of 62-72 hertz which is akin to gamma brain waves. Therefore, the further inward we travel through such practices as meditation the more in tune and coherent our mind becomes with a healthy body.

This type of coherence between mind and body was seen to the astonishment of professor Richard Davidson at the University of Wisconsin when measuring brain waves of meditating Tibetan Monks. Handpicked by His Holiness the Dalai Lama the Monks were asked to meditate on the wish for all sentient beings to be happy. Once the electrodes were in place upon their heads, the Monks settled into meditation. At first the electroencephalogram showed a slowing of brain frequency as the Monks entered alpha and theta states but then their brains launched into the highest frequency of gamma waves. Their brain was not slowing down but speeding up.

Further investigation showed that their minds were not mentally active like seen in high frequency beta waves states but in fact, the entire brain had become coordinated and synchronised. The left and right hemispheres behaved as a unified organ, effectively beaming coherent high-energy gamma waves like a laser.

Psychologist Charles Tart gave himself electric shocks to see if another person in a separate room would show physiological responses to his discomfort. Measurements showed a small spike in the sympathetic nervous system of separated individuals each time he delivered a shock to himself, but when a twenty-minute meditation session was provided for participants before starting, the physiological response was markedly greater. The simple act of meditation increased connection of consciousness and significantly increased the participants ability to 'feel' the shocks Charles administered to himself.

Meditation synchronises and integrates both left and right hemispheres of the brain causing it to become an amplified sender and receiver of energy and information via The Field because all energy is information.

We can witness the power of coherence when the vibrational frequency of atoms in a glass are matched to high frequency sound causing the atoms to oscillate powerfully until the glass smashes. The same harmonic resonance is used to break up kidney stones and has even been used as a weapon.

A healthy body resonates at around 60 to 70 hertz which is very similar to deep meditation gamma wave frequency. Understanding that a healthy and coherent mind produces matching frequencies to that of a healthy body, we can see how mind and body can become synchronised to form a concentrated, coherent and powerful transmitter and receiver of information.

Hopefully it has not escaped your attention that achieving such elevated states of brain coherence via meditation, we are inwardly directing a lot of energy and thus, increase healing and promote optimal physical health. As our body heals and energy flows freely as a result, the frequency of our body increases as we become healthier. At optimal physical health our body and mind become coherent during meditation and a healthy cycle of thriving begins.

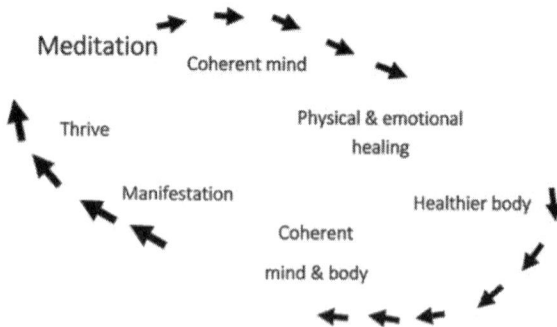

Meditation

Coherent mind

Physical & emotional healing

Thrive

Manifestation

Healthier body

Coherent mind & body

Numerous studies and systematic reviews show meditation to have an immediate and long-term effect on mental and physical wellbeing. In the short-term you can expect decreased psychological arousal, decreased heart rate, reduction in stress hormones and increased positive state of mind. In the longer-term you can expect increased cognitive function, creativity, empathy, happiness, optimism and compassion for yourself and others. Meditation is also found to reduce depression relapse when compared to non-meditators.

With the use of Functional Magnetic Resonance Imaging (fmri), which can view changes in the brain in real-time, neuroscientists can physically see structural expansions occurring within the anterior brain known to be associated with positive emotions during meditation.

Usually the cortical thickness of the brain can be expected to decrease with age along with our mental agility, memory and clarity. However, rather than reducing, regular and long-term meditators are shown to increase cortical thickness regardless of age. Interestingly, the area of the right hemisphere which provides us with a 'gut feeling' also enlarges within frequent meditators causing them to become more intuitive and more aware of extrasensory feelings.

The common link found within all studies of connected consciousness is coherence. Coherence is the unification between mind, body and The Field. A disordered mind is one which is unfocused and without directed attention. Likewise, a disorder of matter is randomness. Because matter is consciousness, it stands to reason that an ordered mind causes matter to become less random and organised towards that which we attend to.

With increasing coherence during meditative practice our mind becomes organised and our body heals. With a healthier body and coherent mind, we become holistically synchronised as a single unit of unified and complete consciousness.

Seminal work carried out by the Institute of HearthMath® shows a coherent body can be attained via the heart. We have an image of the heart having a rhythmical but segregated pumping action heard by the *'lub'* and *'dub'* of values in upper and lower chambers closing as they contract. However, both upper and lower chambers of the heart are stimulated by the purkinje fibres which send an electrical flow from upper heart to lower heart rather than two separate signals. Therefore, the heart has an action more akin to a flowing pulse which gives out a very strong electrical signal. In fact, the electromagnetic field produced by the heart is sixty-times greater than the brain.

Knowing that the heart is a much stronger beacon for energy (measured to expand more than a meter outside the front and back of the body) HeartMath® research focuses on increasing heart coherence more than coherence of mind. Meditation is once again the vehicle to create heart coherence and there are many mediations to choose from.

Buddhist meditations often mention *breathing into the heart* and many other spiritual practices focus on the heart chakra. One such meditation is to begin focusing on the breath – making sure you breath diaphragmatically to stimulate the Vagus Nerve and thus, switch off the sympathetic nervous system – before bringing your attention onto the heart once settled.

Like ripples within a pond which are in synchronisation with one another causing the ripples to become stronger and larger waves, when in coherence with the heart via meditation our entire body becomes 'tuned in' and harmonized. Through this process we become a single, whole and unified transmission of energy which can connect to The Field and thus, also become an open channel for receiving information from The Field too.

CHAPTER 15

PLUGGING INTO THE ENERGY

Dr Barbara Fedrickson at the university of North Carolina found that even novice meditators become better able to cope with daily hassles and stressors. Meditation provides an increased ability to remain within the moment and thus, avoid negative thoughts of past or future and release from second world attachment. Meditators gain an improved sense of self and life purpose. Meditators are shown to feel more compassionately, improving their patience and understanding towards others which, in turn, forges stronger loving relationships. These positive benefits, shown to be accomplished from even modest amounts of meditation, provide improved health, happiness and overall wellbeing.

Meditation also brings the body into coherence and connect with the first world reality. Deep within the present moment during meditation the second world view disappears as we let it go and become the substance of the first world; we become a beaming light of pure consciousness. Principally we become plugged into the first world reality, the world of conscious energy, and become one with all things. In this state there is no time, no past or future, no 'I', no physical body, no house, car or worries, it is a complete state of bliss where spiritual experiences are had and the ability to influence second world reality can be attained.

I still find it somewhat astounding that science is only now helping us gain insight into this truth when ancient Sanskrit scrolls dating back nearly three-thousand years elude to the fact. One such example is that written by Nagarjuna (a student of Buddha Shakyamuni) which reads:

"When real and non-real are both absent from before the mind, nothing else remains for the mind to do but rest in perfect peace"

In a high state of coherence within meditation, we enter through the quantum door, blend with the unified field and experience first-hand the ultimate truth.

From fmri imaging we know that the amygdala, which is largely responsible for the concept of self in relation to separate objects, switches off during deep states of meditation. Thus, with no amygdala creating a sense I', the self disappears, and we become one with The Field. This is also a significant point of coherence known to amplify the reception and transmission of information.

Through coherence we become entangled

All matter is in continuous communication at the level of The Field. All matter is connected via an omnipresent wave of energy and reacts to intentional thought. As with all things, your mind too can become integrated as part of this energy and thus, can influence physical matter from a distance via focused intention.

As discussed, for most of us we are swept along by life and our mind is cluttered from the louder left-hemisphere. An untrained mind is like a bustling train station at rush hour. The rushing current of commuters hastily march through your mind from all directions. Without coordination, you catch parts of conversations, questions, thoughts, ideas, schemes and plans. The relentless chatter and noise fills your mind like whizzing cars on a busy motorway. Imagine attempting to speak with a friend across the platforms amongst this cacophony of sound. You would not easily get their attention little lone connect with coherent communication. In this familiar situation, your unsynchronised mind significantly reduces your ability to focus intention towards goals, desires and aspirations and the message sent across the fabric of first world reality is unclear and therefore, the connection, communication and ability to influence is equally weak.

Imagine the same scene at a train station, but now your mind is trained. As you focus your mind the disharmony and chaos dissipates until all that is attended to is you and your friend standing on the opposite platform. You call their name without the need to shout and they can speak to you with ease and clarity. Communication is clear and direct. In the same way, through meditative practice, you can communicate directly with that which you wish to attract and manifest for your health, knowledge and happiness. Meditation is the direct phoneline to the energy field.

There are five meditative progressions you can expect to journey through when increasing your connection with the unified Field.

1) Analytical thought: Much like you are doing now by reading this book, at first you must use your mind to learn, build knowledge and understanding to form possible beliefs. For

example: "perhaps it is possible I can change my life completely"

2) Experience: You must practice what you learn at every opportunity and apply effort to behave in ways which will help you confirm your newly forming beliefs via personal experience. For example: "I felt a connection when meditating and things in life do seem to be improving for me."

3) Practice patience: The greatest hurdle and biggest downfall on this journey is to destroy your progress because things are not happening fast enough for you. Think of it like a test of your commitment to your intentions. The biggest exam you face will be to remain focused with a steadfast belief in your ability to influence, attract and manifest your wishes and desires. When you think of quitting due to a hurdle or challenging situation, this is the real test to see if you are serious enough to hold onto your belief.

4) Feel more than you think: Work on getting your old limiting beliefs, toxic behaviours or negative thoughts out of your way and just feel. Release

attachment to allow yourself to connect during meditation.

5) Believe: This is the point of no return. Once you truly believe that you are the programmer of your destiny and you are one with all things, magic and sparks will begin to fly. You will marvel at the multitude of things, people and circumstances which provide you with the life intended for yourself. For example: "I know without any doubt that there is no 'I' and the true nature of reality is The Field of emptiness through which my future can be manifested as I choose"

CHAPTER 16

SIX DELUSIONS

As you start out in meditation you are likely to come across six delusions of mind which you will need effort and patience to overcome.

1. DELUSION OF ATTACHMENT

The first is delusion of desirous attachment to second world objects which we discussed previously.

2.   DELUSION OF NEGATIVE EMOTIONS

The second is the delusion of anger and its associated negative emotions which are incoherent and therefore, opposed to unifying with The Field. Anger is a delusion of mind because it is not based on first world reality but firmly fixated within the second world of objects, attachment and illusions of past and future.

Getting angry about something which is happening within our current life or during an event achieves nothing but to harm ourselves and keep us attached to the second world. Anger is an emotion we project onto external objects as if they possess the emotion when the feeling is actually caused by our own mind and created within our own body.

Since an incoherent angry mind is firmly rooted in the second world reality it is heavily based on the illusion of past and future. We get angry about things which have happened, or we get angry about things which may happen, neither of which ultimately exist because the past has gone, whilst the future is yet to come. Both are fabrications of a deluded uncoordinated mind.

In the mist of anger, we can lose control and act recklessly because our mind is uncontrolled and disorganised. This disorganisation disorientates us, and we lose sight of wisdom and even the distinction between right and wrong.

The more you can connect with The Field via meditation the less you will experience such delusions as your mind and body become increasingly coherent. In the meantime, the practice of patience will help release your mind from anger. If you feel anger arising within you, rather than reacting to it spontaneously, practice patience and contemplate the absurdity of this destructive and beauty destroying emotion. Again, this takes effort at first but effort, as you will read shortly, is the key component to your spiritual and personal growth.

3.   DELUSION OF PRIDE

The third delusion of mind is pride which is a state of mind that puts ourselves at the centre of importance when, in truth, we are ultimately the same universal energy and consciousness as all things.

Deluded pride is therefore incoherent because it is firmly attached to the second world reality of separation. The second world appears to our mind as a collection of separate and independent objects when, in the first world, there is no "me" and "you", "us" and "them" or "this" and "that".

Deluded pride is inflated self-importance and therefore not the same as being proud of achievements or being proud of your ability to attain a higher state of wellbeing through effort. Be proud of such achievements and give yourself praise but keep your ego in check always.

4.   THE DELUSION OF IGNORANCE

The fourth deluded mind is ignorance, or as the philosopher Alan Watts more accurately calls it, "Ignore-ance".

If we do not meditate and experience the first world reality we remain ignorant to it and continue to reinforce our attachment to the second world. If you read this book, or any similar book, which presents you with a direction towards the ultimate goal in life, but you do nothing and take no action, you will retain a deluded mind of ignorance and never experience anything more than what you already know.

5.   DELUSION OF DOUBT

The fifth is deluded doubt which is you may need to overcome. Doubt in the belief of attaining an alternative future, doubt of a first world reality or doubt in your self will cause a mind which is uncertain and unable to attain coherence because thoughts, beliefs and behaviours are misaligned. With a mind full of doubt, you are unlikely to put in the effort needed and you will remain ignorant to what is possible.

6.   DELUDED VIEW

And lastly, the sixth delusion of mind that you may have to overcome is deluded view. Deluded view is a mind which obstructs your progress towards the ultimate goal by maintaining a second world view. One such deluded view is that the 'I' is inherently existent and that you (or your egoic-self) is fundamentally separate and individual. As discussed, you and all objects in the second world reality are not independent from each other but rather interdependent upon your consciousness. Consciousness is the entity which brings all things into existence and it is consciousness which can therefore perceive them truthfully as part of The Field. To be able to see and experience the unified field directly through meditation is a non-deluded view.

CLEARING LIFE OF PROBLEMS

Through regular meditation the appearance of deluded attachment, negative emotions, pride, ignorance, doubt and view, will disappear and your mind becomes skilled at attaining their opposite.

- When free from aggression and anger we gain patience and peace.
- With the attainment of patience and peace we are free from resentment.
- When free from anger and resentment we gain kind speech.
- With the attainment of kind speech, we become free from jealousy and gain the ability to feel genuine joy for other people's success and happiness.
- When free from jealousy we are also free from miserliness and gain the ability to let go of second world attachment and the associated worry.

- Now free from attachment and worry we become less guarded and more open and accepting of oneself.

- Having a positive self-concept, we become free from pretension and gain more humility and likeability.

- With a positive view of oneself we gain the ability to accept mistakes and improve personal development.

- With love and acceptance of oneself we let go of self-grasping and the egoic concept of 'I'.

- Letting go of self-grasping we gain a more meaningful prioritisation of what is important such as connection to The Field and spiritual growth.

- As we now grow spiritually we begin to develop more kindness and compassion for all sentient beings.

- With a deeper level understanding of kindness and compassion our behaviours become aligned with our thoughts and we act in ways that support our life and the life of others.

- This in turn provides more meaning and purpose to life and we gain an increased level of engagement with life.
- As our mind, body and emotions become positively aligned towards virtuous actions we become freed from second world distractions and gain increased ability to become more coherent.
- With more coherence comes the increase of energy levels, health and vitality.
- With a coherent mind and healthy body our ability to direct thoughts with intention significantly increase as both mind and body sing as one.
- At this point you will see rapid positive changes within your life.

POTENTIAL BARRIERS

If you were free from aggression, you can see how this would provide more patience and inner peace. Similarly, if you were free from negative self-concepts you would not worry so much about what others think, you would feel contented with who you are, the way you are.

No one in their right mind would choose anger, jealousy, pretension, or any other mind perpetuating delusion at the expense of the opposite life enhancing qualities such as inner peace, self-acceptance, compassion, personal and spiritual growth and so forth.

However, there is one common issue which may hold you back and this, as always, is a barrier within your mind.

Often, we desperately wish to be free from a negative state, however, the question to ask is: What won't you be able to do when you no longer have this negative state?

What won't you be able to do when you no longer have anger?

What won't you be able to do when you are no longer spiteful?

What won't you be able to do when you no longer have attachment? And so on.

If we find it hard to overcome anger for example, often, there is something we believe we are gaining from holding onto such destructive problems of mind. For instance, being free from aggression may mean we have to forgive someone or no longer blame your current behaviour on a past situation, person or event. Letting go of our pretensions may mean we have to give up some of our time or inconvenience yourself for the benefit of others. We may hold onto the belief that being free from second world attachment means to not care or not love in the same way.

Once settled within meditation analyse and notice how you feel. If you feel a negative emotion arise, resist becoming attached to it by attempting to push it away and just let it sit with you in meditation.

Insights into this emotion will come to you and thus, allow you to resolve and let go of it.

Remember, this does not mean you should focus on the negative thought or emotion, but simply notice its presence before returning to The Field within the here and now. All answers to everything can, and will, be found within The Field.

To help you overcome such mind-barriers and get yourself into a more coherent state of brain wave, hypnotic trance can be very useful. Various audios can be found on my website to help you: *wisemonkeytraining.co.uk*

CHAPTER 17

USING THE ENERGY

When connected to The Field via meditation we become one with all things. In this state of pure consciousness and coherence we can send out intentions for the amelioration of life. This intention brings order within our second world and we manifest that which we intend to experience.

Ordering from the cosmos, the law of attraction, or whatever you like to call it, your ability to connect and attract the life you desire, the health you want and even the material possessions you aspire to, can be drawn towards you by connection through the 'quantum door' via mediation, belief and focused intention of thought. All of which takes effort.

Many of the people I have spoken to - usually those who have watched the film *The Secret* - have the idea that all they need to do to manifest and attract their desired life is to have an awareness of what they want and then sit back and wait for it to turn up. However, it is important to recognise that there are key elements needed in place for manifestation to be effective.

The key elements are:

- Belief: You must believe you have the power to attract your ideal life.
- Meditation: Connecting to The Field via meditation is a sure-fire way to transmit your message clearly.
- Intention: Focused intention to attract your future life creates coherence and therefore a strong and clear message.

- **Emotion:** You must feel the positive emotions as if you have already attained your ideal future life.

- **Effort:** All the above involves effort. It is important to recognise the difference between passive wishes, which relies on an outside force, and active wishes, which relates to our own mental intention to bring about our wishes. As effort is needed for active intention we shall briefly elaborate on the function of effort.

Around 700AD a Buddhist Monk called Shantideva at Nālandā Monastic University in India, wrote a book which is now widely known as, *A Guide to the Bodhisattva's Way of Life*. Within this astute text Shantideva talks about four main types of effort which I feel are still insightfully relevant.

The four types of effort are:

1. Armour-like effort

2. Effort of non-discouragement

3.   Effort of application

4.   Effort of non-satisfaction

1.   ARMOUR-LIKE EFFORT

We often think the road to successful attraction should be easy, hassle free and direct like a roman road which takes us straight to our destination, when in fact, it is a winding road with many distractions, sacrifices and even hardships. Therefore, we need to cultivate Armour-like effort which is a courageous mind that perseveres no matter what adversities or distractions may be presented.

Most parents will already know this type of effort as they behave like ferocious warriors to provide for and protect their children. Parents will dedicate a huge amount of effort to secure and guard the wellbeing of their family. Similarly, for attraction, you must have this type of intensive drive and unwavering mindset to meditate regularly and direct your attention, intention and positive emotions towards your desired outcome. The things you need to do and practice to create ideal conditions for affective manifestation should be non-negotiable within your mind.

You must be aligned in mind, body and spirit which is the "Armour" that protects you against external obstacles. You are the superhero of your life, the spiritual warrior who has Armour-like effort in pursuit of the ultimate goal of harmonious existence.

It is helpful to write down the following and repeat it verbatim each morning:

I will continue to practice even if it takes many years. I will never give up, no matter what difficulties I might encounter.

2. EFFORT OF NON-DISCOURAGEMENT

Our biggest obstacle is usually ourselves and therefore you must also develop effort of non-discouragement. The negative voice within your mind may discourage you from time to time, it may tell you that it is too hard, it may create doubt or that you are unable to meditate for example. To overcome these personal challenges, you must develop effort of non-discouragement which is a mind that does not accept or tolerate such negative self-talk.

3.   EFFORT OF APPLICATION

Clearly, for us to attract our ideal life into the physical second world reality we must meditate regularly to evoke the appropriate positive emotions and train our mind to develop positive belief filters. In other words, we need to take action and apply ourselves to such practices.

At times, certainly initially perhaps, we may need to force yourself, which is fine for the short-term or as an infrequent measure to safeguard your consistent practice, however, this is rarely sustainable, so it is imperative to pace yourself.

Planning to meditate for an hour each day from the outset may not be achievable, especially if you are not accustomed to meditation, so pace yourself with small achievable steps. Apply effort of application to construct a daily plan to gradually increase your mediation practice and any other practice you need to structure for your progress.

4.   EFFORT OF NON-SATISFACTION

This effort is a mind directed *towards* the ultimate goal rather than *moving away* from our current position in life. This has been discussed previously and the difference I hope is now understood.

As you practice regularly your life will start to become more organised and you will feel better in numerous ways, but we should not become complacent. Each time a part of your journey manifests and falls into place, this should encourage you to continue. Remind yourself that you are not moving away from where you are but moving towards the ultimate goal. Remind yourself that it is your own efforts and practices which are creating the positive changes.

When you have successfully attracted your desired outcome, it will not end there of course, you will not wish to stop because the blissful, spiritual and mystic experiences you gain from your meditation practices will be a delight for you. Even before your manifestation requests are fully met, you will feel an increased sense of connection and compassion with all sentient beings and will therefore also use your practices for the betterment of human and animal kind.

Through the effort of non-satisfaction, not only will you attain the ultimate goal for yourself, but you will find yourself contributing to the shift in global consciousness and manifestation of happiness for all sentient beings too.

CHAPTER 18

EFFECTIVE MANIFESTATION

From your own experience you may recognise that what you say does not always match with what you truly believe, and this creates incongruence and often dis-ease. What you believe at a deep level holds more power than what you say and therefore, an individual can verbally claim that they are the creator of their own reality as a mantra but if the underlying belief it not convinced, this latter belief will win every time. It is therefore vital to have deeper beliefs which support your personal development and ability to resonate with The Field. With supportive, deeper level beliefs established, your thoughts and behaviours will be aligned. Simply saying you want to attract and manifest will do little if your beliefs, and therefore, thoughts do not match.

"While proper use of consciousness can bring health to an ailing body, inappropriate unconscious control can easily make a healthy body diseased"

Candace Pert, 1997 in Molecules of Emotion

Through learning, understanding and experiencing the true nature of first world reality via regular meditation, your beliefs will strengthen. With effort, meditation practice and patience, your manifestation request will become clearer and the healthy, optimistic and joy fulfilling messages sent inwardly and outwardly will get louder.

When you meditate frequently and start to experience more of the benefits, beliefs about yourself and your potential will strengthen and thus, the catalyst for deeper level changes and attraction will ignite.

So, via the connection with the universal consciousness, the process of order and attraction will physically manifest your wishes and desires, if you adhere to TEN RULES.

NEVER involve specific people. Wanting to attract specific people into your life for anyone's benefit or gratification does not work for four reasons:

- Individuals may be set on a different direction or life journey to your wishes.
- Individuals may not want or share the same wishes, dreams or desires as you.
- If you did attract an individual into your life, who's to say you would make each other happy?
- Even if your motives are noble and you think it would help another person, you can never truly know the potential consequences of your manifestation on someone elses life.

If you are in a happy relationship which you wish to keep, you must involve your partner in your desires to make sure you want the same otherwise there may be conflicting futures being manifested.

For example, you may wish to live in another country as part of your manifestation whereas your significant other may not want to move to a new country. When the opportunity to live in your chosen country manifests itself you will either take the opportunity thus risking your relationship or you will have to turn the chance down.

GENERIC wishes for others. SPECIFIC desires for yourself. You must not aim influence other people's lives unless it is to heal. You should only influence and adjust your own life. So, place generic 'orders' for a collective group, such as wishing peace and happiness for all sentient beings, however, be as specific as possible with your own wishes and desires so the message is clear.

Forget about time frames. The larger your wishes the longer it will take for all elements to be pulled into place for it to manifest so practice patience and do not get caught up with setting time frames. With diligent effort your dreams will come true but only when the time is right. If you were to build your own house, there will be many people, plans and actions needed to setup and prepare before you see any physical evidence of the building. Equally, if the changes you wish to attract into your life are particularly different to where you are now, you must allow the appropriate length of time to pull things together for you, and you have no way of knowing how long this may take, so always practice patience.

Have REALISTIC expectations. I have heard so many people dismiss the principle of attraction and manifestation because they do not understand these rules. For example, wishing to win the lottery is the same message being sent out by millions of other people on the same day at the same time.

With so many identical wishes being sent on a regular basis creates a cosmic queue within The Field and yours will be one of many hundreds in line. With each lottery draw a new queue is formed and thus, you are unlikely to get to the front within your lifetime. So, wish big but avoid queues by making your wishes bespoke to you.

FEEL the Emotions. As mentioned in an earlier section of this book, to really get things moving one of the key elements is to feel the positive emotions you would gain from attaining your ideal life. Feel the deep gratitude, the joy, freedom and happiness as if you have already attained the outcome.

Forget about HOW. You may find yourself asking how your dreams will become your second world reality, but this is likely to lead to discouragement and delusion of doubt. Forget about how it is all going to unfold and just practice the elements laid out within this book to bring it into appearance.

STAY IN LINE! In a world where instant gratification is expected and demanded, we need to be very careful not to become impatient and give up. You cannot make your manifestations move faster by becoming frustrated or impatient, in fact, the impatient message being sent out is the very thing which will delay it. By stating that your wishes are taking too long to materialise is essentially telling the process to take longer. You cannot jump the queue, so once your 'order' has been placed you must be prepared to stay in line to collect it. It is therefore crucial to get your message right from the very start and work out exactly what is it you want, specifically what it will provide you with, what it looks like, sounds like and how it will make you feel. Get this right and clear from the start to prevent continued changes in message.

STICK to your original wishes. What would happen if you ordered a meal in a café but then changed your mind whilst waiting? The chef would have to stop all preparations, scrap your previous order and start again and send you to the back of the queue. People continually change their minds about what they want, especially if it does not happen quickly enough. So, if you want your wishes and desires to become a reality, think hard about what you want, beam the message brightly and stick to it.

BE CAREFUL WHAT YOU WISH FOR. This is your life we are talking about here so please take your time placing orders that will be of benefit to you and those around you. Think about the consequences of your orders. Think hard about what you would like to manifest and attract and what potential impact it will have on your life and those around you? Are you prepared to go through what you need to for your dreams and desires to come true? Who will be affected by the changes that will come? Are you prepared for the changes yourself? Because if you stick to these rules, they will come to true.

The TEST. Things in your life will start to change and this can be tough, difficult and even upsetting. Be prepared for this and see it as if The Field is asking you how much you really want it. See it as a test to see if you stay in line. As difficulties and challenges arise with change, use Armour-like effort to continue.

In a world of "6-weeks perfect abs", "4-day fat loss" and instant access, we are conditioned to want things today, or better still, yesterday. The more impatient you are the more disconnected to The Field you become and therefore, the longer it will take for you to cultivate and experience bliss and attraction. If you are impatient and frustrated with your progress, you are not at one with the conscious field and you risk falling back to a 'sleeping' state of "ignore-ance" by separating yourself further away from the first world reality.

Remember, there is no 'I' but only the truth of universal consciousness. Consciousness is the 'I' and you are one with all things so to demand "I want" or "I need" is to miss the point and reinforce the separateness between you and all things.

For example, if you want to experience inner peace, what do you think you will experience if you force or demand inner peace? Of course, you will become less peaceful and more irritated. This harks back to the concept of attachment which was discussed earlier in this book. There is a paradox in attaining what you wish for because you must let go of wanting it for it to materialise. You must simply practice the content of this book in the knowledge that it will appear. Even letting go of attachment itself can be mentally 'sticky'. If your mind is obsessively focused on letting go of attachment you are attached to it both mentally and emotionally.

This is the essence of letting go.

- ✓ Let go of trying to force things to happen.
- ✓ Let go of attempting to make things manifest.
- ✓ Let go of all endeavours to attain the ultimate goal.

Simply practice, believe and experience without expectations or forced desires and you will move at a greater pace toward your development. When it comes to attraction and manifestation, remember to feel more than you think. Feel the gratitude, feel the connection, feel the peace, feel the love, feel the happiness as you meditate. Simply be present in the moment, let go, practice patience and experience.

All too often life does not turn out as we wished because our mind is scattered, we are rarely in a state of coherence and too busy focused on the multitude of second world distractions. When asked what your ultimate wish in life is, the mind may gravitate to all the things you want to eliminate which does little to answer the question and certainly does not help to move you towards your ideal existence. Because of this, we rarely have a definitive and concise idea of what it is we ultimately want, what the outcome of our desire is or even what our life would look like once achieved. All we tend to be aware of is that life should be better or different to how it is. The vague, mixed and often changing message we send out can be thought of much like sending a letter of communication. In this scenario all we address on the front of the letter is what we do not want with no other details.

This creates a three-fold problem. Firstly, as previously explained, a 'move away from' mindset will only help to provide limited and brief reprieve.

Secondly, the unconscious mind – which is the ultimate driver of intention – can only take direct commands and therefore does not differentiate between 'do not' and 'do'. For example, right now I do not want you to think of a tree. I *do not* want you to think of the leaves blowing in the breeze. *Do not* think of this tree.

Your mind responds to the command within a message and negates the rest to hear "think of a tree" rather than "do not think of a tree". So, when you state all the things you do not want in your life, the picture in your mind, the emotions you feel, and the thoughts created are directed towards the very thing you do not wish to manifest.

And thirdly, with such a vague address on your manifestation 'letter', at best, it will take a long time to reach its destination, or, more likely, it will float aimlessly around the ethos.

Once again, it is vital you are absolutely clear on what you do want. Think about it in detail so the picture within your mind and the emotions you feel are positively directed towards rather than away from. This message will therefore have a full address, zip code and even directions.

Note: It is worth highlighting that during meditation you should initially practice training your mind to become focused at your command rather than using it as a means to manifest as this will hinder your progress. Remember, at first your disobedient mind will be unfocused and muddled so meditation at this stage should be aimed at cultivating a mind which becomes more synchronised, able to work at a higher frequency and magnify focused intention. Once you feel as if you have attained better control of your mind, during meditation you can visualise your desired future, create a clear image within your mind and feel the positive emotions as if you are already there. This skill will enable you to send direct messages out whilst connected during meditation.

AIDING YOUR MANIFESTATION

Professor Karl Pribram and David Bohm theorized that if we could block our senses we could learn from The Field directly and intuitively. By blocking our senses, we would decrease mental distractions and thus, support access the first world reality. Sensory deprivation studies suggest that Pribram and Bohm were correct.

Intrigued by consistent reports from experienced meditators of a conscious power to connect with all things, parapsychologist Charle Honorton, Psychologists William Braud and Adrian Parker, independently set out to investigate such claims. Knowing that a common factor cited was the need to decrease 'mental noise' to aid mental focus Honorton, Braud and Parker used a deprivation method called the 'ganzfeld' or, 'whole field' technique.

Their experiment involved splitting couples into separate rooms where one was to receive a telepathic message sent from the other person. The receiver was asked to put on noise cancelling headphones, listen to relaxation music to help put them in a focused trance-like state, and wear blackout glasses to remove vision too. To prevent the receiver getting too relaxed and falling asleep, they were asked to continually report what they were experiencing until told otherwise.

Meanwhile in a separate isolated room, the sender was asked to select a few boxes from a pile. Within each box was a number and those picked were entered into a computer which in turn randomly selected one picked number. This number corresponded to a picture which was shown to the "sender" on a screen and asked to mentally send the image to the "receiver" in the other room. To help them stay focused, a picture of the receiver would intermittently appear on their screen. After thirty minutes the session was over.

Removing the head phones and glasses, the receiver was presented with numerous pictures, only one of which was the one being sent to them by their partner. The receiver then chose which picture they believed was being sent.

Knowing that what they were about to investigate would be met with cynicism, before these studies were carried out, Honorton, Braud and Parker made sure they learnt from the flaws and mistakes of previous investigations, and thus, ensure the results they found could only be caused by a non-local connection between sender and receiver.

Calculations showed that the receiver was likely to pick the correct one by chance once every four sessions. However, a meta-analysis of twenty-eight studies showed that in fact, the receiver successfully picked the right picture nearly every time.

These studies indicated that, with the right conditions, novice individuals with no previous meditation experience have the capability to send information via The Field and increase their ability to receive information too.

Knowing that sensory deprivation can significantly aid our ability to connect to The Field as a sender and receiver, you may choose to find a sensory deprivation floatation tank in your local area. As part of your practice, you may also choose to wear headphones whilst listening to hypnotic audios, to move your brain wave state towards Theta and Gamma, and watching a visual representation of your desires whilst listening.

A highly effective way to add substantial power to your manifestation is to use *mindmovies.com*.

This Mind Movies Creation Kit is one of the most powerful online tools for personal development and visualization in the world. To date they've reached over 2.1 million people and is highly recommended by influential figures such as Bob Proctor, Dr. Joe Dispenza and Dr. Joe Vitale to name a few.

Create your future today at *mindmovies.com*

CHAPTER 19

ULTIMATE TRUTH

This book has the aim of laying out the path to the ultimate goal of lasting happiness via the ultimate truth of reality and human potential. The Darwinian theory of human evolution lacks the addition of consciousness and therefore is focused on physical strength and aggression whilst dismissing virtuous attributes such as altruism, kindness and compassion. Advances in the science of Positive Psychology show that such virtuous traits broaden and build positive psychological, physical, social and cultural strengths. Rather than a separated view of "survival of the fittest" we now know that to really evolve, today it is about a unified thriving of the kindness and happiness.

When Professor Martin Seligman and his students sifted through numerous text from a variety of religions – some dating back three-thousand years – they found six virtues common to all. This book has aimed to meet these very same virtues:

1. Gaining wisdom and knowledge through personal and scientific enquiry.
2. Having the courage to direct effort, intention and challenge limiting beliefs.
3. Developing love and humility by decreasing separation and increasing unity and oneness.
4. Developing an increased sense of justice by seeking equality and compassion.
5. Having temperance through the development of patience, non-attachment and self-mastery.

6.   To reach outside of self, connect with the universe to access higher purpose and transcendence.

The direction of human evolution has always been to discover and connect with The Field. Within The Field, via meditation, our right hemisphere of the brain comes forward and unifies with the dominant left helping us feel more connection rather than think more about separation. With a coherent heart, mind and body we can receive and send information via the universal energy of consciousness, which is the ultimate truth of reality. At this point we all become entangled with one heart and mind to create a blissful, peaceful and harmonious second world reality for us all to live happily.

Professor Rich Snyder states that being hopeful and optimistic about the future is a combination of belief in ones' ability to attain the desired goal and the intention to reach this destination. I hope you can now recognise that you do indeed have the ability, not only by your own efforts to change unhelpful or limiting beliefs, thoughts and behaviours but also via meditation to connect to the universal field of consciousness.

No longer can we assign our undesired progress in life on our personality, hereditary characteristics or other people because we are in control of our own destiny.

On reading the following quote, I have imagined the astrophysicist Carl Sagan sitting behind his desk having read the last of many research papers on the quantum nature of the cosmos and reality, leaning back in his chair a saying with a smile:

"Somewhere, something incredible is waiting to be known"

FURTHER BOOKS & RESOURCES

WiseMonkeyTraining.co.uk

Best wishes

Anthony

Printed in Great Britain
by Amazon